Dear Von,

May God b

The Best is yet to come!

Much Love

God Spoke
and He fulfilled it

Kiril & Angelina

From every prophetic encounter through each defining moment, Kiril and Angelina Istatkov lead life with Spirit-inspired purpose and passion for God. When I first met them, I could clearly see their relationship with God as their source of drive, direction, and destiny. This book, *God Spoke — And He Fulfilled It*, comes at a relevant prophetic season, revealing worldwide revival and global harvest fields. Every story testifies of how real and faithful God truly is to orchestrate their lives — from their perseverance through persecution to significant personal sacrifices towards the convergence of their destiny — to align towards the great revival emerging today. Kiril and Angelina are living their divine calling. Their personal experiences, displayed first-hand through their humility and determination, will certainly inspire and uplift you.

Che'Ahn
President and Founder, Harvest International Ministry
International Chancellor, Wagner University

Kiril and Angelina have a story that looks a lot like the book of Acts. Living ordinary lives in the midst of a dead religion, only to encounter a Power they never knew existed, Who catapulted their family into a life of impossibilities made possible and a journey much like the apostle Paul. This couple is the real deal, and as their apostolic covering, we see every day a couple in love with Jesus, determined to spread His love through the demonstration of signs, wonders, and miracles. Their autobiography is a story that increases faith and serves as a reminder that we serve a God of details and promises kept.

Mark and Patricia Estes
Senior Apostles
North Charleston Apostolic Center

In an earlier era, J.B. Phillips famously diagnosed our modern condition with this dramatic assessment: "Your God is too small." Sadly, that malady has not improved for the vast majority in our society, so Kiril and Angelina Istatkov have made it their mission to right that wrong. By being raised in a homeland where material possessions were in short supply, they were forced to trust completely the only One with the power to meet their real needs. As a result, they believe in a great, big God. I've heard their story face-to-face and have been blown away by their faith. As you read it in black and white, you will see things that run the gamut from the mundane to the miraculous. As they recount in these pages the unbelievable, their love for the Lord and each other is unmistakable. Thanks be to God.

Dondi E. Costin, Ph.D.
President, Charleston Southern University

God Spoke — And He Fulfilled It is a must read for every believer in Christ Jesus. Kiril and Angelina Istatkov share their journey of stepping out on nothing except a promise from God and seeing Him fulfill it. This incredible couple are true, end-time revivalists, bringing the fire of God accompanied with great signs and wonders. This book will inspire you, ignite you, and cause you to run into your God-given destiny.

Debra George
Debra George Ministries
www.debrageorge.org

Upon first meeting Kiril and Angelina Istatkov, I immediately felt that we were kindred spirits. Their story, told in this book, is a tale of one miracle after another. As you read, you will see that their amazing gifts are truly from God, yet they humbly act as conduits of God's love to all people. I count myself blessed to be their friend during this amazing time of revival in the world.

Daniel Carpenter
Pastor, Palmetto Land Baptist Church
Summerville, South Carolina

God Spoke

and He fulfilled it

THE STORY OF REVIVALISTS KIRIL AND ANGELINA ISTATKOV

Angelina Istatkov

God Spoke — And He Fulfilled It
The Story of Revivalists Kiril and Angelina Istatkov
ISBN 978-0-9916124-8-2
Copyright © 2018 Kiril and Angelina Istatkov
P. O. Box 22572
Charleston, SC 29413

We dedicate this book to Hope, our dear Nadezhda, who has walked with us through most of the events of this book. She is not only our loving daughter but also our powerful and faithful partner in ministry.

Contents

INTRODUCTION

There is a difference between hearing about God and hearing Him speak to you. You can learn about His character and His will, but there is nothing like knowing Him personally, being led by Him as He reveals himself to you. You experience His love, His faithfulness, and His protection, and you also find that He is a strict Father! He will correct you, instruct you, and discipline you because you are the apple of His eye. You discover that He is perfect and holy, and nothing sinful can stand in His presence. Our God is love, but He is a consuming fire as well.

The moment I heard Jesus died for my sins, I realized how much He loved me. I realized how much God loved me, that He gave His only Son for me. Giving my life to Him was the beginning of a glorious journey and life in the Spirit, an experience in which God has led me and changed me. In the beginning, it was difficult to imagine what God had planned for me, but I had a deep trust that He would unfold His plan a little bit at a time, and I would see His glory. I didn't know how it was going to look, but what I knew for sure was that my life would never be the same.

That's what this book is about — my life with Jesus, with Kiril and our daughter, and with our wonderful brothers and sisters in Christ. Everything you will read in this book, everything He has done for us, He wants to do and will do for you. Give Him a chance, and watch what He will do. You will see how much He loves you too!

1

KIRIL'S EARLY YEARS

I will begin our story by telling you about a great man of God, my husband Kiril Istatkov. It is not boastful to write about him, because he is God's man. God made him what he is and what he is becoming. Kiril is a prophet, not because he calls himself a prophet, but because the work of the Holy Spirit through him defines him as a prophet. From the time he was a small boy, Kiril sought after God and wanted to serve Him; but you could say that his calling chased him until he was born again and began to flow in it.

Kiril was born on March 20, 1966, in Sofia, the capital city of Bulgaria, Europe. He was the youngest child in a middle-class, working family. This is significant, because the tradition in his parents' family was to only have two children. They had a baby girl first, but she died a few days after she was born. Two years later, a son was born, and Kiril was born four years afterwards. Kiril may not have been in his parents' plan, but he was in God's plan!

Kiril grew up in a peaceful, harmonic atmosphere. When he was between the ages of six and nine, people would ask him what he wanted to be when he grew up. He would always say that he wanted to become a priest, a man of God, but he graduated high school with a major in electronics. After that, he went into the army for two years. In communist Bulgaria, every eighteen-year-old boy went into the army for two years. While he was serving in the military, Kiril prayed, sought, and trusted God to be with Him with the knowledge and understanding he had from the Eastern Orthodox Church.

Because he didn't want to carry a weapon in the army, God miraculously changed his position to a communications operator. Being polite, kind, and excellent in his job, he earned the respect of the generals and the commanders in the army. After his two years, Kiril continued his education for two more years in the evenings. During the day, he worked in a factory making computers. It was a well-paid job, and he was earning more than his mother and father combined.

One evening, Kiril was on his way home on the bus. At one of the bus stops, a man in a suit and black coat sat down next to him. At the same time, some of Kiril's friends from high school came over to him and asked how he was doing. Kiril told them how he tried to manage his life between work in the factory during the day and school in the evenings. He also mentioned some of the problems at the factory, that it was a stressful atmosphere and he was very dissatisfied working there.

After his friends left, the man sitting next to Kiril told him that he was the executive director of the factory called Elektronika Ad, an electronics company in Sofia. He asked Kiril to meet him in his office on Friday. The man explained that his car had broken down, which was why he had had to take the bus home.

Kiril went home and shared what happened with his parents. His mom became very angry. She was scared Kiril would be fired from the job he had. She was also angry because he dared to speak in public about the factory where he worked. At that time, people were afraid to speak what they thought in public about politics, government, or anything about the society. Under communism, people were not allowed to speak openly about anything important, including religion and where they worked.

Despite his mother's anger and fears, Kiril showed up that Friday in the office of the executive director of Elektronika Ad. He gave Kiril a better position with a higher salary and in a much better atmosphere. The only people that worked in those positions were people who had very close connections with the authorities in Sofia.

Bulgaria was a communist country from 1946-1989, with a president who was a dictator and in office for thirty-five years. We were taught in school that there is no God and that we became humans as a result of evolution (similar to Darwin's theory). If anyone proclaimed to be a Christian, they were excluded from the Communist Party, lost their job, their kids were not allowed to go to school, and they lost every benefit the government provided. Christians were treated as traitors to the country, and they usually ended up in a labor (concentration) camp. Some were there for a lifetime.

Once, Kiril was called to the police station to explain why he received mail from Western countries, such as France, Italy, and Spain. He was writing letters to actors and singers across the border, asking for their pictures with autographs. He was collecting them, but he had to tell the police what was in the letters. If you have always lived in America or a free country, you cannot imagine the kind of control the communist government had over us at this time in Bulgaria.

Nevertheless, everything seemed to go very well in Kiril's life. He went out every weekend to disco clubs and loved to dance. He never smoked cigarettes or drank alcohol, but he was paying for his friends' drinks, and he was always the center of attention. He made sure he always looked good and had a tailor sew his clothes. He celebrated his birthdays in very expensive places and could afford to go on vacations to Eastern Germany and Czechoslovakia. He visited historical places there, as well as museums, castles, and many places a young socialist did not go. He was friends with the most popular musicians and singers at that time in Bulgaria. He had all their albums, signed by the artists. He was welcomed to their homes, and he was always at their concerts.

On Easter, a few people were permitted to kiss the hand and receive a blessing of the priest in the Orthodox Church. Kiril always was one of them.

2

KIRIL IS CALLED TO MINISTRY

In 1989, six months before the communist government fell, Kiril visited an evangelical church for the first time. During that time, the church was underground, as it was not approved by the government. The people met in a very poor, small gypsy home. The senior pastor, Pavel Ignatov, was persecuted all the time. He was arrested a few times by the police and taken to the radioactive mines, where he worked without protective clothing. They were trying to turn him away from the faith he had in God and to deny Jesus, but he stood firm. After a while, they didn't know what to do with him. Every day after work, they measured the radiation on his body, and it was much lower than the other miners who wore special clothing and helmets. God was glorified!

The pastor was the only person in the evangelical church that had a Bible. There had not been Bibles in Bulgaria for fifty years. The people would listen to the sermon during the services, but when they got home, they did not have access to any Christian books. It was a time of great persecution, but also a time of great visitations from the Lord. Praise the Lord for His Holy Spirit! He would remind the people what they had heard in the service and reveal Jesus to them in amazing ways. Jesus spoke the truth: "But the Helper, the Holy Spirit, whom the Father will send in My name, He will teach you all things, and bring to your remembrance all things that I said to you" (John 14:26).

Some of Kiril's friends stopped coming to Saturday night disco, and he asked them why. They told him they had started going to a church. One of them asked, "Do you believe in Jesus Christ?"

Kiril said, "Yes."

His friend then asked, "Do you believe He died for your sins?"

Kiril answered yes again.

His friend said, "Okay, so you believe Jesus came and died for everybody's sin?"

Kiril said, "No, He didn't die for everybody, but only for special, good, and nice-looking people like me."

His friend explained that Jesus' sacrifice on the Cross was for everybody, so they could come to God and be saved. Feeling like he couldn't argue with Kiril anymore, he invited him to go to the church meeting with him. Kiril decided to go.

The church met in a home in the darkest, dirtiest, poorest place of the city: the gypsy neighborhood. The police rarely went there, and if they did, the Christians would say that the reason for their gathering was a wedding. Kiril wondered why the Christians were so poor, why the women had to cover their heads — and why they were so happy! They joyfully sang songs to the Lord. If God was with them, why did they have to suffer this way?

While he was thinking all that, the presence of the Lord came so powerfully over him. God touched him and assured him that He was there, that He loved everybody — the poor, the needy, the intellectuals and educated people — the same way. The love of God captured Kiril, and he gave his life to Jesus.

In June 1989, Kiril was baptized with the Holy Spirit and began speaking in tongues. God put him with people who were very firm and strong in the Lord and who operated in the gifts of the Holy Spirit. Some of them had been active prophets for forty or fifty years in ministry. God poured out the gifts of the Holy Spirit in Kiril and started to speak mightily through him. He was taught how to listen to God, to be obedient to the Lord, to fast, and to pray.

Most of the knowledge he got was given to him by the Holy Spirit before he ever read the Bible. When Kiril had his own Bible for the first time, he read in it all the things the Spirit of God had been speaking to him! The same Holy Spirit that dwells in us is the same Holy Spirit that wrote the Bible. In the beginning, God spoke to him about his life. Later, He began to speak to him about others around him in a prophetic way.

In Bulgaria, there were few prophets in that time, and one of them was Brother Stephen, an older man. He had heard from the Lord that he was supposed to go to Sofia and find God's child, Kiril, to pray for him, to anoint and ordain him. Brother Stephen had served the Lord all his life, during the persecution of the church. He was in the office of a prophet, and God had done a lot of miracles through him. When he heard from the Lord to go to Sofia and find somebody with the name Kiril, he went there and started asking the Christians, "Who is Kiril? Where is he?"

One evening, at a home group gathering, Stephen and some other older ministers of God were gathered together for prayer. Kiril knew about this gathering and that the prophet was looking for him. He was afraid to meet him, because he didn't know what to expect from him. On his way to the service, Kiril thought the prophet had gone back to his city and would not be at the gathering. He was right. They did not meet the first time Brother Stephen came to Sofia to find Kiril.

Brother Stephen went home, but God told him to go again. This time, Kiril arrived at the service and Stephen stood up. He laid his hands on Kiril and anointed him. After that, God started using Kiril to prophesy and perform miracles, healings, and deliverance. One sister was healed from a brain tumor!

Brother Stephen prophesied over Kiril at the end of the service. He said, "In two years, God will take me home [Heaven], but you will not live in Bulgaria anymore." Kiril remembered those words and many other prophetic words spoken to him and confirmed through others. God told him, "You are My prophet, through whom I will do great signs and miracles."

That sounds very good, doesn't it? Kiril thought God speaking through him to His people was a great calling. Every believer loves to hear from God. He had a childish faith and with open arms loved the people. He felt compelled by God to show His love to everybody! But there also was a price. Kiril had to go through hurt, the pain of rejection, the disbelief of others, and persecution from his brothers and sisters in the faith. That was so difficult to understand.

Through it all, Kiril believed in the power of the unity of the body of Christ, and he still does. He began to understand that not everybody who claims to be a Christian is truly a Christian. Not everyone has given their life to God, where they will sacrifice their own desires, agendas, and plans to love and serve the Lord and His people. That was lesson number one, but Kiril never lost his childlike faith and love for people. Praise the Lord!

3

FIRST TIME IN HEAVEN

Just a few months after Kiril received the Lord as his personal Savior, Jesus took him to Heaven. The things He showed him were incredible! He described the moment when he was sitting at a long table across from Jesus. Kiril had his head down on his arms on the table, hiding his face. Jesus said, "Kiril, look at Me."

Kiril answered, "No, Lord. I cannot look at Your face."

Jesus said again, "Kiril, look at Me. Lift up your head."

"Lord, I'm a sinful man. I'm not worthy to look at Your face!"

Jesus replied, "Whoever I have forgiven and set free is free indeed." Then Jesus stretched out His hand and lifted Kiril's head so he looked at Him face-to-face! He has tried so many times to describe Jesus to me. He has blue eyes. His hair reaches His shoulders, but He looks so different from the paintings and drawings we've seen.

As they were sitting at that table in Heaven, Jesus spoke to Kiril about the calling He had for him, "I will do great signs and miracles through you. You will travel around the world and bring salvation to millions, but know that all that is My work through you. So now, I will show you what you should rejoice about."

Jesus took him to another place and showed him the Book of Life. He opened the Book and showed him his name written with golden letters. "This is why you have to be happy and to rejoice in Me, because your name is written in the Book of Life. Everything else, the signs and the miracles, they are My work."

Kiril asked Jesus, "Lord, what about Peter, my brother from the church I go to? What about him? Is his name here in this Book?" The Lord opened another page and showed him Peter's full name and the place and time he was born. Kiril asked about some other people he knew in the church. The Lord told him, "Not everyone you know now will be here with Me. There are some people around you who love you, but they do not love Me. But I want you to promise Me something. I want you to promise that you will always speak My Word, the truth, no matter what it costs you." And Kiril promised.

After Jesus took Kiril to Heaven, Kiril shared it in the church. The presence of God came so mightily while he was sharing about his experience with Jesus. When he told about seeing his friend Peter's name with his place and time of birth in the Book of Life, the mother of Peter began shouting and praising God, confirming his place of birth. Nobody knew Peter was born in another city, because his parents were on a trip when his mother had to give birth. The Lord was encouraging the church to trust Him, to believe that Heaven is real.

4

REVIVAL AMONG THE GYPSIES

After God revealed His will and the purpose of his ministry to Kiril, He allowed tests and trials to come in his life to perfect his faith in Him. Long times of fasting and praying became Kiril's lifestyle. The anointing and guidance of the Holy Spirit increased, and He started to lead him even for the very little things with details.

Eight months after Kiril received the Lord, he went to this little city called Varshec in the mountains. It was known in Bulgaria for its spa centers. He went there with a few brothers and sisters in Christ. God sent him with his team (who were primarily gypsies) without telling them why; but later on, they found the purpose behind it. When they arrived there, they found a very small group of Christians. This was right after the fall of communism, so most people had never heard about Jesus Christ and the message of the Cross. This local church had only ten members, who were all family members of the pastor. It had been like that for ten years. Nothing new was happening.

When Kiril and his team came to the church, it looked like a home group. Kiril prophesied boldly to the pastor, "I see you, Brother, as a shepherd with a shepherd's cloak, and I see behind you a lot sheep; and God says, 'In three days, I'll give you a lot of sheep, many new believers.'"

The pastor was thankful for the word, but he was skeptical. He said, "Kiril, you are very young in the faith. That's why you speak such things. I believe God will increase the number of the church, but in three days? You are so enthusiastic, you will calm down soon."

Kiril didn't know what to say to him. He sounded so discouraging. The next day, while Kiril and his team were walking in the city, they met a few gypsy women, who were sweeping the streets in the park. Kiril and his team started speaking to them about Jesus, and God began working in their hearts. The women came that evening to the church, and they were very hungry to hear more about God.

During the prayer time, Kiril heard from God that he was supposed to go to this certain lady's house the next day in the gypsy neighborhood to minister to the people there. But he said to the Lord, "Lord, I cannot just invite myself. How will I go there?" While he was talking to God, this lady looked at him and asked him if he could come the next day to her home and share the Word of God with her relatives and friends. Praise the Lord! Kiril didn't need any other confirmation. He was ready to go where God sent him.

The next day, when the pastor realized Kiril and his team were getting ready to go to that gypsy area of the city, he was very worried. He said, "Kiril, you are crazy if you do that. Do you know that nobody goes among the gypsies? Even the police don't have control there. They can kill you there!"

Kiril replied, "Kill me? If this is God's will, I am okay with that. But Brother, I'm sure God spoke to me to go and to share the love of Jesus with these people, no matter what it is going to cost me." The pastor's daughter also decided to go with them, so the pastor told them that if they didn't come back in two hours, he would come with the police to get them out.

Filled with the faith, power, and anointing of the Holy Spirit, they went into the gypsy neighborhood and strange things started to happen. As they were walking the street, looking for the house of that woman, a group of men approached them, cursing them and saying all kinds of ugly words. They came closer to them, obviously intending to harm them. Kiril lifted up his arm and commanded the devil to leave, and the whole group of men stood there frozen. They couldn't move, so the team continued on their way undisturbed!

When they arrived at the house of the woman, there were already many people inside and outside the house. They had come to hear about God. Kiril and the team started worshipping the Lord in gypsy language. The people were so touched by that, because Kiril was a Bulgarian singing in their language.

When Kiril saw how many people were gathered, hungry to hear about God, he started to cry. He asked the Lord what he should tell the people, because he hadn't even read the Bible yet (at this time he didn't have one). While he was praying this, they had to move into the back yard, because there was no more room in the house for so many people. God told Kiril, "My son, just open your mouth and speak, because not you but I will speak through you."

Kiril hadn't been to a Bible school or even owned a Bible, but he was still in the school of the Holy Spirit, which is the best school! As he spoke to the people, he listened to what he was saying. It was one of the best messages about the Cross he had ever heard! People began crying and were deeply moved. He asked them to start praying. They lifted their hands. Then one young man asked Kiril to stop the prayer, because he wanted to say something. At first, Kiril remembered how his pastor had taught that only the devil tries to stop you from praying, that it is not right to stop. But then God told Kiril to stop the prayer and allow the young man to speak.

The young man said, "I see a man with a white robe walking among us, and he is laying his hand on everyone here. When he came to me, I asked him, 'Who are you?' and he said, 'I'm Jesus Christ.'"

The presence of Jesus in that back yard was so awesome and tangible. Such powerful conviction from the Holy Spirit came over everyone that prostitutes, homosexuals, and murderers fell on their knees to ask God for forgiveness. One woman said that she has practiced black magic to make her neighbor die. She said, "I'm so sorry for what I did. What should I do now for God to forgive me?"

Kiril told her to go to her neighbor, confess her sin, and ask her to forgive her, to hug her and tell her she loves her. Then he told her to bring all the magic materials to the meeting. Other women also confessed to using black magic, and they all ran to bring their occult books of spells and curses and other objects. When they returned, they burned every evil thing, and they heard voices scream from the flames and then die away.

The love of God took control of the whole crowd of people. He began restoring families, mothers, fathers, and children. Suddenly, Kiril noticed a young man in the crowd. He was looking at him with a very serious expression. Kiril was ready to go to him, but the others stopped him, telling him that he was a dangerous man, a murderer. Kiril went to him anyway, hugged him, and said, "Jesus loves you, and He wants you to come to Him and to follow Him. 'Your wife and children ran away from you, but if you come to Me,' says the Lord, 'I will bring them back to you.'"

At first, the man stood like a stone, because nobody knew what had happened with him and his family. Then he burst into tears, fell on his knees, and repented, confessing Jesus Christ as his Lord and Savior. The Holy Spirit came so powerfully with one touch from Kiril or his team, the people started speaking in tongues. God ignited the fires of revival in the gypsy area of the city of Varshec. Between three and four hundred people were saved, healed, and baptized in the Spirit of God. The revival meetings continued three days in a row, and each day, more and more people joined the services under the open sky, as God saved many people and did many miracles.

On the third day, right before the end of the gatherings, Kiril saw Jesus coming from the fields. He was coming closer and closer until suddenly, Kiril couldn't see Him anymore. "Lord, where are You? Where did You go?"

Then he heard from inside him, "I'm in you, My child."

At the same time, a cart with horses arrived. Riding in it was an old, paralyzed man. He had a long beard and smelled bad. His sons brought him after they heard about the miracles of God. They asked Kiril, "You said that there is nothing impossible for God, right?"

Kiril answered, "Yes, there is nothing impossible for my God."

They said, "If it is so, please pray for God to heal our father, who has been paralyzed for fifteen years."

Now that was a big challenge for Kiril! He asked all the people to stretch their hands and to pray for the man in the cart.

God spoke to Kiril, "I want you to hug the man and pray for him." He obeyed the Lord and walked over to the cart. He stepped into it and hugged the stinking man, closing his eyes.

Then he commanded the unclean spirit to leave this man. Afterward, he stepped back, lifted his hands, and started giving praise to God. He didn't look back to see what had happened with the man, but the people began crying out. Someone tapped his shoulder, and he turned around to face the man he had just prayed for! He had stood up and was trying to walk!

Everyone was amazed and giving praise to the Lord. Great joy came in the household of this man. Because of his testimony of the healing miracle, forty members of his family immediately came to Christ. Before Kiril left, this man told him, "Kiril, I have two cars. I want to give you one of them."

Kiril replied, "I don't need your car, brother, but always let your heart belong to Jesus. Give your heart to God and serve Him faithfully."

After the three days of revival meetings in the gypsy area, the prophetic vision was fulfilled. All the people that received the Lord attended the local church, and this is how God gave that pastor a lot of sheep in three days. Kiril, his team, and the pastor saw how God's ways are not like our ways, and His thoughts are not like our thoughts. We know partially and prophecy partially, but God is leading us in a victorious procession. When we are faithful, everything He promises, He will fulfill in His time, in the way He wants.

Through His glorious visitation in the city of Varshec, God began to reveal to Kiril how his ministry would look in the future. He increased Kiril's faith and zeal to serve Him more.

5

REVIVAL IN ELIN PELIN—AND I COME ON THE SCENE

Most of the young people around Kiril at that time were from the town called Gara Elin Pelin. A small group of evangelical Christians would travel about an hour to Sofia to attend The Bulgarian Church of God. They stayed in home groups and had home services, and God spoke to them a lot, edifying and teaching the believers. In Gara Elin Pelin, the Holy Spirit was moving mightily, and the group started to grow. God gave them favor with the mayor, who allowed them to have their meetings in the city hall for free. Kiril led the services once a week. A team from another church joined them to lead the worship.

The Lord started to do His works and miracles. Kiril was giving place to the Holy Spirit, who spoke through him in prophetic words, visions, and words of knowledge. He didn't preach long messages. More time was spent in worship and moving in the gifts of the Spirit. People also shared their testimonies and the joy of experiencing healing and deliverance, which increased the faith and expectation in the people's hearts.

I was sixteen when I first went to church in my town of Pernik. I went just out of curiosity. I had heard that the people there spoke in languages even they didn't understand, that it was a gift from God to talk to Him directly. Thankfully, I heard not only the people speaking in tongues but also the message of the Cross. I knew in my heart that from that moment, my life belonged to my Savior, and my life would never be the same.

I was told that when God forgives my sins, He writes my name in the Book of Life; and, as confirmation, He will send His Holy Spirit to dwell in me and I will speak and pray in heavenly tongues. I was excited to hear about being born again, baptized in the Holy Spirit, and speaking in tongues.

After I heard about Jesus and the Holy Spirit at this meeting, I went home. My parents and my brother saw that I was not the same. There was no bitterness in my heart. Instead, there was forgiveness. They knew me as a very closed person, because I grew up with both parents being alcoholics. My father and mother were drinking a lot, and there was no peace in my home. The fear of death was very much present in me at a very early age. I hid my mother's butcher knives every night before I went to bed, because my parents were fighting. Many times, my father threatened to kill my mother, my brother, me, and then himself.

Growing up, I had so much hate in my heart for my father. He was always angry with me, so our communication was very poor in my teenage years. At the same time, I felt sorry for my mother, who was a workaholic, and the alcohol was her enemy. Many times, she would be drunk in the bathtub, and I was so afraid she would kill herself. She was a pretty strong woman, but she had been deeply hurt and disappointed in her life. I grew up with the shame of having such parents, because everyone in the neighborhood, our friends, and our relatives knew our story.

Very often, after my parents came home from work and were drunk, they would argue. We lived on the sixth floor, and my father would throw pans and plates out the window while I was playing with other children from my building outside. It was so embarrassing. That caused me not to have friends. I was very quiet and depressed. The only place I could find comfort and approval was at school. There, I knew that if I had knowledge,

I would earn the teacher's approval and the other children's respect. Other comforts were food, the television, and Michael Jackson's songs.

Growing up during communism, I was told there was no God. I believed this, but deep inside I also believed there was love and light and a different life. I just didn't know where to find these things.

After that first church meeting, I came home and said to my father, "Daddy, I met Jesus! He saved me. He loves me. And He loves you and wants to save you too!" I had not called him Daddy in years. I was so excited, happy, and filled with God's love. The love shook my father, and he didn't know what to say. He wanted to show anger toward me, but he couldn't deny the love and the change that had happened in me. The love of God flowing through me hit him, and he felt uncomfortable.

I said the same words to my mom, and she began asking a lot of questions. The dramatic change in my behavior touched her so much. God led me to fast and pray for my parents after I truly forgave them. I showed His love and spoke to them about Jesus every day after that.

The day after I met Jesus, I turned off my phone, locked the door to be sure nobody would interrupt me, and went down on my knees. I started to pray to God to pour out His Spirit on me and forgive my sins. I prayed about twenty minutes and then I thought, *Nobody will hear me.* I didn't know that the devil was speaking a lie, and my atheist and unconverted mind was resisting the truth I had heard at church.

Finally, I said, "Lord, I will not get up from prayer until You baptize me with the Holy Spirit and I pray in tongues!" I continued to pray, and after ten minutes, the presence of God came so powerfully in the room. I felt this way for the first time. It was so tangible. I knew I was forgiven, accepted, and loved. I was crying and laughing at the same time, and I couldn't speak in Bulgarian anymore. I was praying in heavenly tongues! Praise the Lord! Unspeakable joy filled me up. That was my first personal experience with God. I knew for myself, for sure, that Jesus was real. He died for my sins, and I was accepted into His kingdom.

After that wonderful encounter with God, I felt the fire of the Holy Spirit so strong on me that I opened the door and ran out of my home to tell the neighbors — the people I was once ashamed around and afraid to talk to — that Jesus was alive, and I could prove it! Later, after I read the Bible, I realized I had felt like the disciples when they received the promised Holy Spirit on the day of Pentecost. God baptized them with His Spirit and fire, as the Word of God says, and they ran out of the Upper Room to share the Gospel with the world. These were those who were hiding just days before — just like me!

At my church, I heard that in a city close to Sofia, God was doing miracles. I had to go and see what was happening there. People were talking about Brother Kiril, how God was using him to speak to the people and do signs and miracles in the meetings. They talked about him with such a respect, I thought that this man must be old, at least fifty years old. I traveled by train to Gara Elin Pelin, and the train was full of passengers who were Christians. They were playing their guitars, singing, and worshiping the Lord. Others were praying for people to receive Jesus Christ as personal Savior. I looked around and said to myself, "O my God, this is the train of glory!"

We got to Gara Elin Pelin, and almost everyone on the train got off. A big crowd headed to the city hall for the service. When I got there, the place was packed. There were probably between four and five hundred people. The atmosphere was filled with the presence of God, and there was such an expectation in the people's hearts to encounter the love of God, to receive their deliverance and healing. I learned that people from all around the country traveled to get to the revival meeting. Even before the service, I heard some amazing testimonies of healing and deliverance that had taken place in previous services.

I took a seat, and right before the service started, Brother Kiril quickly stepped up to the pulpit. I thought, *O my God, he is so young!* When the worship started, the presence of God was so powerful. He gave a short message from the Bible, and then Kiril began to prophesy. For the first time in my life, I heard God speak to His people. It was so clear, specific, and accurate! Every word was spoken with power and was confirmed with the tangible presence of the Lord. I was amazed.

Then I heard the Holy Spirit speak to me for the first time. He said, "This man is going to be your husband." But I ignored it! I still didn't know how God spoke to me. I thought I was imagining it. For a long time, I was afraid to share what I heard and kept it to myself. It was only after I knew Kiril and I were going to be married that I spoke about what the Holy Spirit had said.

At the revival meeting, I was only interested in other people's miracle testimonies. Eyes began to see, and deafness was gone. One lady said that in the last service, she had felt the power of God over her broken arm like fire, so she believed God had healed her. She said she had gone to see her doctor the next day and had asked him to break the cast, because Jesus had healed her. The doctor refused, telling her that she was crazy and that it was impossible. She needed to have the cast on for twenty more days. She insisted, and she had to sign papers that if something went wrong it was her responsibility. They removed the cast, took an X-ray, and saw that her arm was completely healed. Praise the Lord!

During the service a little child about five years old ran up the steps of the platform and ran around Kiril. Kiril asked him where his mother was. The ushers found her, but she couldn't say a word because she was crying so much. When she finally could speak, she said that her boy couldn't walk at all, that he had had two surgeries on one leg and three on the other, and the doctors had told her he would never walk. Now, watching her son running on the platform, she began shouting and praising the Lord. Everyone started worshipping and thanking the Lord for the miracle. We all knew Jesus was alive!

I was very touched and impressed from what I saw and experienced at this revival meeting, but I thought, *Everybody here comes to worship the Lord and to serve the Lord, but I'm so sinful! I'm only sixteen — and I'm thinking about marriage!* So, I decided not to go to these services again, because I was afraid God would punish me for having these thoughts about Kiril.

6

GOD SAVES MY HOUSEHOLD

It wasn't long before some of us started a home group in my home in Pernik, which is about thirty kilometers from Sofia. My mother was very interested to hear every testimony and a lot about God, and I was sharing with her what I had heard and seen. God truly started working in her, but she had to deal with her pride and to come to repentance. She was a strong woman with great influence in her job, and she had a lot of friends, but she was caught in alcoholism and the occult. She was a fortune teller, using coffee grounds. While she worked in a butcher factory, people came to her during the lunch and coffee breaks with their coffee cups. She told them their future under the influence of a spirit of divination, and when she was drunk, the devil used her even more. She told people their past and future, which put them in bondage to evil spirits. Many people at her job, relatives, and neighbors came and brought her money and gifts for hearing their fortunes.

At twelve or thirteen-years-old, I started drinking Turkish coffee so I could ask her about my future, but she couldn't tell me anything. She didn't know anything! God had me even before I knew Him, and my life was hidden in Christ!

One day I came home from church and saw Mom lying on the couch in the living room. When I opened the door, she started complaining about a terrible headache and asked me to call an ambulance. She said she was dying. I don't remember clearly what I said to her, but she told me later that I replied, "I'm not calling the ambulance, and you will die if you don't repent and give your life to Jesus and turn away from your wrong ways. I'm not calling anybody, so you decide for yourself what you're going to do." Then I went to another room and started praying in the Spirit.

Even she was surprised at how I reacted. She felt that the headache was increasing and she was falling into a deep hole of darkness. She knew she was on the way to Hell. Suddenly, she realized it hadn't been me speaking to her but God's warning. He was telling her to surrender her life to Jesus. She came in the bedroom where I was praying and asked me to lead her in prayer, that she was ready to give her life to the Lord. I led her in prayer, and my father came home. He came into the bedroom and laid on the bed.

My mother was repenting and confessing Jesus as her Lord and Savior, and God poured out His Spirit on her and she started speaking in tongues. She couldn't say anything in Bulgarian for the next half hour! When this started, my father jumped from the bed, shaking her and trying to talk to her, but she only would speak in tongues! He was a witness of my mother's baptism with the Holy Spirit, but he was still resisting, saying that we were crazy and that what we were doing was not right. This happened just two weeks after I received the Lord.

My mother and I were excited to follow the Lord, go to church, and get together with brothers and sisters to share testimonies of what God was doing in our lives. My mother became a great witness for Jesus to all the people she had told fortunes to. Now she was preaching Jesus to them and everyone she knew. There was no more alcohol in her life. It happened overnight, and people who knew her were always asking how she was so changed.

About a month later, my father left to go to a spa center for two weeks, but he came home after the first week. He had been drinking that evening, but he was so joyful and wanted to tell us what had happened to him while he was on vacation in that little town. He said that while he was walking in the park, two women started talking to him about Jesus. He looked at me and my mom and said, "I heard the very same things you told me about God! I was running away from Him, but He found me there. I decided to come back home and ask you to lead me in prayer for repentance and receiving Jesus Christ in my heart."

We all went down on our knees, and my father prayed the prayer. Shortly after that, he started speaking in tongues, and there was no more alcohol in him. He was completely sober! Even the smell of the alcohol disappeared. From that day, alcohol was gone from my home. Praise the Lord! God's peace came, and that was evident to the whole neighborhood and everyone who knew us. People started coming to our home meetings to find out what had happened. The number coming to our home group was increasing, so that eventually every week we had about forty people.

One day, when we were meeting, I opened the door to see Kiril and a lady from our group. She was his neighbor in Sofia and had invited him to visit our meetings, as he was traveling around the country at that time. When I saw him at my door, I thought about how he was a powerful minister of God, and I didn't know what to expect from him as a person. I thought he might behave like a Hollywood star, but I had the good surprise to see him approach everybody with the love of Jesus and have normal conversations. In our meeting, he shared the Word of God and gave prophetic words with such love and care. He prayed for everyone individually, and when he came to me, I was amazed. He spoke things that were only between God and me. I felt like this man had been in my prayer closet!

Even as a new believer, I was still an introvert and very closed off. I did not share with others what was really going on inside me, my worries, my questions, and my concerns. It was difficult for the people around me to reach me. When the Holy Spirit started speaking to me through Kiril, I was completely disarmed! Everything in me, all the questions that I had, all the worries, and every prayer I had prayed was revealed through him, and I was completely shaken. I thought I knew God, but at that moment I felt like I knew nothing!

Don't misunderstand me. I did not feel like the Holy Spirit was "telling on me." He's not a gossip; He is a gentleman. Although I was stunned hearing God's answers coming out of Kiril's mouth, I felt God was so close, real, and true. He cared enough to send Kiril to speak to me, to put my heart at ease.

Then the Holy Spirit said something to me that, at first, I didn't understand. He said, "Why don't you believe Me?"

In my thoughts I answered, "Lord, I believe in You. Why are You are asking me this question?" Then I realized He was pointing to something He had been telling me for almost a whole year. I knew I would have to deal with it.

7

DEALING WITH WITCHCRAFT

As a new believer, I had come under the influence of a sister in Christ, who operated in the gifts of the Holy Spirit, giving prophetic words, words of knowledge, and healing people. She started good, walking with the Lord, until she allowed sexual sin to come back in her life and committed adultery. She ended the affair but hid it, thinking that it was enough for her to repent to the Lord in private, that it wasn't necessary to confess her sin and be healed.

James 5:16 NIV tells us, "Confess your sins to each other and pray for each other so that you may be healed." Sin does damage to our lives, and we need to be healed when we turn from it. By confessing it to a pastor or another brother or sister and receiving prayer and encouragement, we receive real spiritual deliverance from the effects of our sin. Unfortunately, this sister did not do that, and she became mean, prideful, and controlling.

This woman still operated in the gifts of the Spirit and thought she was hearing from God, but her heart was not right with Him and she was hearing the enemy. She lived in Sofia and came to our home group, where she began to lead the meetings. One day, she shared with me her vision to register Christian Association for Peace and asked me to help her. At seventeen and so new to the Lord, I became her secretary. I was very excited to do this for God and embraced the idea of starting something bigger in my city that would bring more people to Christ.

Everything was good in the beginning, but after a few months, I started feeling bad spiritually. Every time she prophesied a word from the Lord, I would start crying and didn't know why! The evil spirits of Jezebel and witchcraft were operating through this lady, and the Holy Spirit in me was grieved every time she did. She took control of the services in my home and began speaking against pastors and ministers of God. Instead of speaking words of edification, exhortation, and comfort (see 1 Corinthians 14:3), she would read scriptures against people who weren't present, even telling lies about them. This is how the Spirit of Jezebel manifests. That spirit always attacks and accuses God's ministers, just like the real Jezebel killed the prophets of God and threatened to kill the prophet Elijah.

After speaking these terrible things, she would take a love offering and go back to Sofia. She also became very close to my mother and began to control everybody in our group. Things really got bad when she started speaking curses over the people who resisted or opposed her. People became afraid of her. She asked the mayor of our city to give her a building to conduct her services. When he said no, she cursed him and prayed for him to be in a wheelchair. One month later, he had a car accident and was in a wheelchair. A lawyer also had a car accident because she cursed him, and she cursed my godmother's son, who had an accident on his job and lost his eyes. He is still blind.

When Kiril came to our home group that first time, the Lord asked, "Why don't you believe Me?" He wanted me to believe what He was telling me about this woman, that she was not right with Him and was doing evil things. By this time, this Jezebel/witchcraft spirit had taken over our home group.

Kiril came to my home a second time, when the lady was not there. He told us that God had revealed to him a spirit of witchcraft and Jezebel operating through this woman. Our group began to pray, and God gave Kiril a word to be told to that lady. It was that she had to repent for her adultery, because she was a married woman with two sons. She was to humble herself and stop judging and speaking evil against the people of God.

That was my first time dealing with people in witchcraft, and it was very difficult; but, at the same time, it was a great learning experience. I was one of the closest to this woman, and she had used me to take over the home group. I was responsible for all these people coming under such deception and demonic attack. Everyone in our group was a new Christian, and the Word of God she taught us was compromised. For example, she taught that if you steal things from your job for yourself, it is a sin; but if you steal things from work to help a brother or sister in Christ, it is not a sin.

After God gave this word to Kiril for this woman, we all agreed that we should talk to her and correct her. When we did this, she first began to cry. She saw we were determined that we would not tolerate her behavior anymore. Then she became angry, saying that she was okay and didn't have anything to repent about. She refused to confess her sins and left the meeting in a rage. She was cursing us, telling us we were all going to die. Gangs would attack us, and she was going to report us to the police.

She wanted to stop us, but we became even stronger, standing on the Word of God. The question God had asked me through Kiril was, "Why don't you believe Me?" God was not only talking about what I believed about this woman, but the fact that all the words she spoke over me did not come true or line up with what He was telling me. The Holy Spirit was teaching me to listen to and believe Him and not those who spoke words that did not agree with what He was telling me and what His Word said. He wanted me to see that I needed to have confidence that I was hearing from Him for myself. God showed me the difference between a false prophet and a real prophet when I saw how different Kiril's words were from hers. For one thing, his were accurate and hers were nonsense! Also, his heart was right with God and hers wasn't.

In a week, we had a board meeting, without the president (the Jezebel lady), and we voted her out of her position. Then we went to the court and removed the registration of the association from the register. This is how the enemy's plan was destroyed. Praise the Lord!

The spirit of witchcraft comes to make you doubt your relationship with God and rely more on what someone else is telling you. It shakes the solid foundation you have in trusting God's Word and the Holy Spirit inside you. This evil spirit confused me about who I was in the Lord. I was starting to feel lost and thought God was not with me anymore, because I was so tormented by confusion and deception. Little by little, I was falling into depression. I cried for no reason, and I knew inside of me that something was really wrong.

In the beginning, you think it is your fault. Then you say, "These are attacks of the devil!" When you feel this confusion, you know that does not come from God. And when you cry out to Him for help, He will send brothers and sisters who will help you get delivered from the witchcraft and Jezebel, just like Kiril did for me.

I learned that the devil uses people, even believers, just like God uses people. That's why it is so important to be in a body of believers where the Word of God is taught in the right way and the Holy Spirit is allowed to move freely. Then we can discern what is evil and what is of God. We can hear His warning about coming attacks of the enemy and expose his lies, counterfeits, and deceptions. We can stop him in his tracks!

Isn't it wonderful that, even though I was very new in my walk with God and didn't know the Word of God very well, even though I came under the influence of someone who was not following the Lord, God delivered me and taught me so much through it. He is always faithful!

8

OUR LOVE STORY

When I was saved, I always had been insecure, frightened, and full of complexes. As a child, I was told many times that I would never succeed in my life. I would not be a good wife or mother, I would never learn to cook, and the list went on and on. It is sad, but these word curses came mostly from my family.

About a year after I first heard Kiril at the revival meeting, he began coming to our home group services, and God started changing me very quickly. Kiril taught us from the Word of God, encouraged us to pray and listen to the voice of God, to be obedient to the Holy Spirit, and to learn to walk in the love of the Lord. I had so many questions that I kept to myself, but Kiril would speak words from the Lord that would answer my questions and open me up. As I received the Word of God more and more, it brought healing and restoration to my soul.

In the meantime, God called Kiril to travel throughout the country and prophesy, which he did. He traveled to every city or village the Holy Spirit told him to go. He traveled with a team of two or three believers, and wherever they would go, God would use him to lift up the churches through prophecy and do many miracles. Churches and families that were separated were getting together again, and wounded souls were healed and restored through the powerful words given through Kiril. He didn't know the people who came for prayer, but God gave him accurate details, increasing the faith of the people. He also taught the people how to pray and communicate with the Holy Spirit, and how to live pure and holy lives for the Lord.

As Kiril fulfilled the call of God on his life, one of the places he came to minister on a regular basis was my home group in Pernik. God used him to resurrect my faith and trust in the Lord, but he also taught us how to stay before the Lord and walk in the callings on our lives. He encouraged us in our personal relationship with God. I'm very thankful for the patience and the love with which he explained the Word of God to us, even repeating the same things over and over until it came alive in us. And, it was always a miracle to me when he would say things that I had only told God.

Through Kiril's teaching and prophesying, my faith and trust in Jesus grew fast. It wasn't long before I was saying, "Lord I know who I am in You! I know what You want from me." My great zeal and desire to serve God began to have a purpose. God broke the curses and witchcraft off my life, and I became a completely new person.

During the summer of 1994, Kiril was in my home in Pernik. He was my brother, and I didn't dare think about him as a husband. While a group of us were in prayer, God told us that He was sending us to the city of Ohrid in the Republic of Macedonia. We were to move there. I looked at the map to see where this city was located, because it sounded like Odrin, a city in Turkey. We found that Ohrid was a beautiful city on a mountain lake in Macedonia. We took a short trip to visit Ohrid and find out more about the plan of God, why He was sending us there.

Our team took the bus, and after two hours we got to this high mountain, the border between Bulgaria and Macedonia. While Kiril and I were waiting for the passport control, standing outside the bus, God said to both of us, "Look at this land. I'm giving you this land. I will make you citizens of this country, and I will use this country like a jumping platform for the next season of your ministry. I will prepare you and send you to the USA." That was the first time we heard that God had a plan to send us to the United States.

After we entered Macedonia, we had to travel five more hours on the bus to get to Ohrid. It was such a beautiful place. The people were very friendly, since it is a tourist city. We stayed there a couple of days, and my mother told me that she was a citizen of this new-formed country. It had previously been a part of Yugoslavia, but now Macedonia was an independent country. My mother was Macedonian, and we never knew it before. We thought she was Serbian. We discovered this after God spoke to us about His plan.

On that first trip to Macedonia, my mother, brother, and some other families were with Kiril and me. They thought this was what God wanted for them too, but God didn't speak to them about moving there. He only told that to Kiril and me. I was Kiril's secretary and was excited to share the same vision for ministry, that God was expanding our territory and ultimately sending us as missionaries, first to Macedonia and then to the USA.

One evening, Kiril and I were sitting on a bench next to the lake. The sun already hid behind the mountains, and the street lights were on. We were looking at the peaceful water, listening to the lapping of the waves, and talking about God's plan. Suddenly, I saw Jesus walking on the water, coming closer and closer. I asked Kiril, "Do you see what I see?"

He said, "Yes, it is Him!"

When Jesus was close enough, He stretched His arms toward us and said, "From today on, you are husband and wife. Your life and ministry are one." He also told us that we were going to travel all around the world, and His name would be glorified though our lives and ministry. So, we got married in Ohrid, Macedonia, December 23, 1994.

9

Skopje

A few months after we were married, the Lord told us to move to Skopje, the capital of Macedonia. By this time, in 1995, everybody who had come with us to Ohrid had gone back to Bulgaria, so Kiril and I were by ourselves. Because my mother was a citizen, I was a citizen and could get a job and work. Kiril got his identification card, so we didn't have to leave the country and extend our stay every month; but he was not allowed to work in the country until he became a citizen in 2001, six years later.

We had to make a lot of adjustments to our new city. We expected to see revival take place the same way it had in Bulgaria, with evangelism and many salvations, but God told us that the ground was completely different. He had a different way to reach the people of Macedonia.

Sixty percent of the people were Eastern Orthodox Christians. They were very religious but didn't know Jesus. They were caught in the rituals, the holy days, and the works, which encouraged self-righteousness and pride. Those who attended church faithfully thought they were better than other Christians and other people. God told us, "Tell this people that I'm not with them and that they have to repent and receive Me as personal Savior."

This proved to be very hard. The Word of God had to be taught, and there was great hatred for Bulgarians. The Macedonians had never forgiven the Bulgarians for occupying their country during World War II, when Bulgaria was on the side of Nazi Germany. Now the Lord was sending two Bulgarians to tell them, "Thus says the Lord: Repent, for His kingdom has come!" This was madness to our natural minds, but God had a plan.

We connected to a Pentecostal church, which had been newly founded. The pastor was a local man who, with a Norwegian journalist, started having meetings in a rented theater hall. He had evangelized some students in the university, so the church was mostly young people, who had just received the Lord. There was a lot of immorality and drugs among the congregation, but spiritual pride left over from their religious background was the real problem.

When we started to fellowship with them, they loved the anointing and the move of the Holy Spirit, but the Word of God was too challenging for them. They didn't want to change. It was like they just added Jesus to the things in their lives, and if you observed their lives, they didn't look any different from people who were not saved.

Kiril and I kept reminding ourselves that God had said, "Look at this land. I'm giving you this land. I will make you citizens of this country, and I will use this country like a jumping platform for the next season of your ministry. I will prepare you and send you to the USA." He had brought us to Macedonia for His glory and to prepare us for our ministry in the United States.

While I was working, Kiril was doing ministry in Skopje and in different cities in Macedonia. He ministered in their churches, home groups, and as he was doing volunteer work in some American Christian organizations that were helping the Kosovo refugees in Macedonia. In the city of Struga, MK: Shelter Now, an international humanitarian organization, opened an office in the Muslim area of the city, where a lot of locals were hosting Muslim refugees. Kiril volunteered to help distribute food and clothes to the refugees' families, but he also ministered to the people who worked in the organization and the local church.

One day, someone from the office gave Christian tracts to the children who were playing on the street outside. An angry man with a gun opened the door of the organization's office. Kiril welcomed him, but the man put his gun to Kiril's head while yelling, "Who dared to give my children tracts about Jesus? Allah will reward me in Heaven if I shoot you!"

God gave Kiril peace and a word. "Sir, I have been to Heaven. I am glad to go there again if you kill me, but I know that if you kill me now, you are going to go to Hell. Jesus loves you, and He doesn't want you to perish."

The man said, "How do you know that? Who are you?"

"I'm a prophet of God, and God speaks through me."

The Muslim man dropped the gun and fell on his knees. He was so touched by the Lord and His love. After Kiril talked to him about Jesus and His love, this man said, "I hate my religion. It's all about hatred and killing." He took his Muslim cap, dropped it on the floor and stepped on it. Praise the Lord! This was just one of the many awesome things God did as Kiril ministered wherever He sent him.

While we worked for the Lord in Skopje, the time came for our family to increase. When I got pregnant, we moved back to Sofia to live with Kiril's parents until the birth. On May 27, 1998, the Lord gave us a precious gift: our daughter Nadezhda (Hope). Her name literally means hope, and she was named after my mother-in-law. We were so thankful for our daughter, a healthy and peaceful baby. The doctors said, "She is growing as it is written in the books, everything is according to the books!" A great hope came with her for our future and God's promises for the ministry to be fulfilled.

God gave us our Hope to keep our hope in Him alive. We had the most wonderful time with our newborn girl and enjoyed every moment together. There was a peaceful atmosphere, even though Kiril's parents were not yet turned to God. We knew we were there only for a season, but they wanted to keep us forever. They couldn't understand the calling we had and the ministry God had entrusted to us. They were taking care of us as their son and his wife not as God's ministers. God taught us how to be patient and loving towards them.

Even before she was born, God told us that Hope would be a very smart child, who would bring great joy to our lives, that she would worship God and bring glory to Him. What more could we ask? His mercy is endless! Thank You, Lord, for You have blessed us more than abundantly!

In our family, we had some difficult moments through attacks from people who were standing against God and resisting His Word and the word of prophecy. They rejected the idea that God would speak through us, and particularly any word of correction. They just liked the nice, flattering words. If God spoke anything else to them through us, they spoke evil against us. They went to great trouble to justify themselves and find excuses not to receive the word of the Lord.

The Bible has a lot to say about persecution. It comes to steal the Word of God from your heart (Mark 4:17), from religious people who are jealous of your freedom in Christ (Acts 13:50), and because you are living a godly life for the Lord (2 Timothy 3:12). Jesus said that if people persecuted Him, they would also persecute those who believed in Him and followed Him (John

15:20). He also said, "Assuredly, I say to you, there is no one who has left house or brothers or sisters or father or mother or wife or children or lands, for My sake and the gospel's, who shall not receive a hundredfold now in this time—houses and brothers and sisters and mothers and children and lands, *with persecutions*—and in the age to come, eternal life. But many who are first will be last, and the last first" (Mark 10:29-31, italics mine).

Along with the great blessings from God, we had persecution as well. Some stood against our marriage and ministry, even close people such as parents, relatives, brothers and sisters in the Lord, as well as people from the world. Through all of this, God taught us how to do His will and build our family. He taught us how to forgive and love no matter how we were treated.

When Hope was eight months old, it was time to leave Kiril's parents' home and go back to Macedonia. It was painful for them, and they were grieving because of our leaving. They wanted us to stay so they could watch their granddaughter grow up. We assured them of our love and told them we had to follow the Lord. We said, "If you really love us, please encourage us to go and continue to serve the Lord. It is important to be where God wants us to be, but we will always be your family, no matter the distance."

Coming back to Macedonia in January 1999, God sent us again to the church with the young people from the college. We started to fellowship with them. They came to our home, and we prayed for them and taught them the Word of God. God wanted to bring change, to awaken them to the delivering power of the Holy Spirit and drive sin out of the church. We spoke the true word of the Lord at every opportunity. We showed them the love of God, but we never held back the truth from them.

God is the same always; He does miracles now as He has

always done. One day, a young man and his girlfriend invited us to go to a picnic. When they came to pick us up, the girl's twenty-five-year-old brother was with them. They had invited him for a reason. While we were at the mountain to have the picnic, they shared his story. He had been addicted to heroin for five years, was a Satan worshipper, and had been diagnosed with Hepatitis C. The doctors gave him just a few months to live. He looked like a walking dead man: pale, lifeless, scared, and depressed. At the church, he was saved, but people told him he was a dying drug addict. No one prayed for him to be healed, and he didn't expect to be healed.

His sister asked Kiril to pray for him, and she asked if her brother could live with us for a time. Our daughter was one year old, but we agreed; and his parents brought him the next day to our apartment. We didn't know anything about drug addiction or what he was going through, but we knew that nothing was impossible for our God. Whatever demon was tormenting this young man, it had to go in Jesus' name. Right after he got to our home, the young man flushed his methadone down the toilet, and the battle started.

The prayers were intense, with the power and authority Jesus had given to all believers. Kiril prayed for the man to be delivered of all demons. The first change we saw was that his appetite came back. After a few days, his cheeks turned red, and he wasn't pale anymore.

Kiril cared for him as a son, surrounding him with a lot of love and making him feel secure. The young man was a tattoo artist, and he still had his tattoo studio, where people mainly from the underground and drug dealers were his customers. After receiving Jesus Christ, he felt delivered from the business of selling drugs. People from the mafia became angry with Kiril and me for taking one of their main dealers away, and they were angry with the young man as well. Kiril went with him to his studio, because there were threats on his life.

One day, some guy from the mafia came in with a gun. He put the gun to Kiril's head, and only God saved him. Kiril spoke to the man about Jesus, and he put the gun down and left. Two weeks later, Kiril went with the young man to the hospital for his regular check-up. The nurse took his blood and noticed a visible change in his veins. Previously she had had trouble inserting the needle and finding a vein, but now they were visible and full of blood.

As they were waiting for the results, they noticed that next to the desk were many laboratory test results of different patients. The young man was curious and saw a paper that said, "Hepatitis C negative." He thought to himself, *God, this is somebody that just came here, did the test, the result was negative, he takes his paper, and goes home; but I'm dying!* While he was deep in thought, the lady from the desk took that paper and handed it to him. He couldn't believe that this was his. This was a miracle! He was healed! The Hepatitis C was gone! They went to his doctor with the test results. She knew his situation very well and was shouting in amazement, "This is impossible!"

Glory to Jesus Christ!

God not only delivered him from drugs and the mafia but healed him from Hepatitis C and gave him a new life. We went to the church and showed the paperwork — before and after. It was a testimony for believers and unbelievers. The doctors in the rehab center and every medical institution knew about that miracle. The whole city knew that Jesus delivers and heals the hardest cases!

When Kiril and I saw God do these amazing miracles for the people, no amount of persecution could defeat us!

10

CIVIL WAR IN MACEDONIA

God spoke to us when we first came to Macedonia, "Live among these people, but do not become like them. They think I'm with them, but I want you to tell them that I'm against their pride and I'm calling them to turn to the Lord their God." God was calling His people to come back to Him, repent, and live holy lives. Many received the Word of God and started serving Him with all their hearts, but there were a lot of others who didn't want to hear. They were in spiritual pride and told us that we spoke against them and didn't love them.

We were surrounded by Christians who wanted revival to come to Macedonia, and they had put a lot of hope in a Christian man from Strumica named Boris Trajkovski, who was from a family of Methodists. When he was younger, he and his family lived in the United States, and he returned to Macedonia with a desire to help his country. He got into politics and was recognized as a very charismatic person. During the Kosovo refugee crisis that began in the spring of 1999, when many Albanian Muslims poured into Macedonia, he was the minister of foreign affairs.

He had the attention of the citizens of Macedonia and earned their trust, so he became a candidate for president in the next elections. The fact that he was a friend of George W. Bush, who was running for president of the United States, gave hope to the people that he would bring change to the country.

Evangelical Christians were excited that he was a Protestant and would do a lot for them, that the Eastern Orthodox Church would be weakened and revival would come.

This sounded good, but God said that this wasn't His way of bringing revival. He said it would start in the Church, preaching the Gospel of Jesus Christ, and that believers bring change in a society. Spiritual change first; then natural change. Change comes from the preachers not the politicians. When we shared this with the church, they didn't want to hear. Again, there were accusations against us.

Boris Trajkovski was elected president in November 1999, and many evangelical Christians thought he would be the savior of the nation. They thought he would solve every problem, but his term was marked by tensions between the ethnic Macedonians and the large Albanian minority, mostly Muslim, who lived mostly in western and northwestern towns.

The Albanians, who were a little over 20 percent of the population, were angry because they were no longer allowed to fly the Albanian flag and their language was no longer considered the second language of Macedonia. In fact, they were forbidden to speak it in public places, including schools and universities. In the past, they were treated as partners in the government, but now they felt disrespected and dishonored.

One day, Kiril had a vision. He saw black birds coming from the north (which would be Kosovo) over the country. God said that He would crush the pride of this nation and bring them to repentance. This was a warning, but the people in the Church didn't want to hear. They said we hated them because we were Bulgarians. Kiril warned them that a war was coming, but they insisted that they were a peaceful nation. Macedonia had peacefully separated from Yugoslavia, so there was no chance for war to happen. There was so much resistance to the word of the Lord, and few people believed what God was revealing to us.

On January 22, 2001, a group of armed Albanians attacked the police station in the village of Tearce near Tetovo, killing a police officer and injuring three others. The Albanian authorities in the Macedonian government criticized the attack, but then a group of Albanian Muslim terrorists, called the National Liberation Army (NLA), claimed responsibility and began to attack more towns on the border of Macedonia and Kosovo. In response, the Macedonian army went to fight the terrorists and take back the villages, but the NLA had everything planned in advance. While the Macedonian army fought for the first border villages, the NLA captured other border villages. The civil war had begun. It was also a war between the Muslims and the Christians, because Albanians in Macedonia were mostly Muslim and Macedonians were mostly Christian.

While the Christians in Macedonia had been fighting among themselves and with other Christians in neighbor countries like Bulgaria, Serbia, and Greece, the NLA had been planning to take over western and northwestern villages in Macedonia. This is how much the people in Macedonia were blinded by their pride. God knew and tried to warn them, but they wouldn't listen.

The capitol of Skopje, where we were living, was shaken. The terrorists were everywhere, but you couldn't tell the difference between the peaceful Muslim population and the terrorists. In the mountains, there were shepherds that became a weaponized para-army. Walking in the city was dangerous. There were explosions of trash containers, and we needed to trust God for protection. Only ten kilometers away from downtown Skopje, the Macedonian army was bombarding a village of five thousand people. Fear and insecurity took over the whole country. The news reported dead policemen and soldiers, and the nation was in mourning.

God's people were protected in this time of suffering. He was providing for us, for every need and even more, just as He promised in His Word. We remembered that He had told us, "The plagues of Egypt will not touch you." This was a promise from God! He told Kiril and me that while Macedonia would burn in a war, we would be protected, and He would bless us. He told us, "If you can make it in Macedonia, you can make it everywhere!"

Still, it was hard to watch. We saw with our eyes that pride brings destruction. The same thing happened to Israel and other nations in the Old Testament. Every time Israel's heart moved away from God and they disobeyed Him repeatedly, He had to remove His hand of protection and allow Israel's enemies to take them captive. God always warned Israel through His prophets, just like He warned the Macedonian Christians.

During that time, our families and the Christians in Bulgaria pressured us to come back to our country, but we knew we had heard from God where we should be. We knew that if we returned to Bulgaria, we would crumble spiritually, our family would fall apart, and we would not hear from God. We knew that the safest place to be was in His perfect plan, no matter how dangerous it looked. We were confident that He knew what was best, that He loved us, and we could trust Him for everything. When we do this, we can glorify Him with our lives and bear good fruit for His kingdom.

Many of those in Macedonia, who had stood against the word of the Lord before, apologized and asked for prayer when they saw Kiril's prophecy happening. These Christians saw that when God was telling them to repent of their pride, He was only trying to save them from the destruction that came in the civil war. They saw that His warning was out of love not hate, that the word of the Lord we gave them was out of love and not hate.

We all learned how important it is to consider every word of prophecy, even if it is a hard word that calls us to repentance. We should put away all offense, go to the Father, and ask Him to show us what we need to know and what we need to do. If the word is false, He will tell us to disregard it; if the word is true, He will show us how to be delivered from destruction and be saved and blessed. As we walk in obedience, He will empower us to do His will, to stand and believe His promises for our lives.

And so, we stayed in Macedonia and continued to trust God to protect us and empower us to continue to minister to the Macedonian people. They were so terrified because of the daily clashes and the bombings. Our daughter Hope had just turned three, and God told us to pull her out of kindergarten. We did that, and a few days later something amazing happened while she was sitting on her training potty. She started glowing and sweating. We asked her what was going on, and she answered, "Mommy, Daddy, I hear somebody speaking inside me!" We asked her what she was hearing, and she opened her mouth and started speaking in tongues! God baptized her with the Holy Spirit!

We praised the Lord for that great blessing, that our daughter would experience the work of the Holy Spirit at such a young age. We remembered that six months before this, Hope had had another encounter with Jesus. After her afternoon nap, she walked into the living room, and we saw her face was shining. She said she had seen a man with a white robe. He came to her, hugged her, and told her that His name was Jesus. He said He loved her very much. She was His child, and she would praise

Him and serve Him all her life.

These things occurred when we were going through great persecution and trials. On one side, the devil was trying to discourage us, to bring fear and doubt so we would stop walking with God in His plan. We were very tempted to go back to Bulgaria. When our little girl spoke these words that she had heard from Jesus, we began to praise Him for this visitation of encouragement. And now she was speaking in her heavenly language! God was showing us that He had everything in His hands.

President Trajkovski presided over the NATO-brokered peace deal in July of 2001. The civil war was over within months, and God had seen us through the crisis to give us peace and security.

Through the years, God has spoken to Kiril and me about each step of His great plan for our family and our ministry, and there is always a warning. He will tell us how the enemy will attack, tempt us, and try to get us off the path of blessing He has for us. He will tell us that there will be difficult times, hard times, but He will see that we come through them if we follow Him. He always tells us in a very serious and firm tone how important it is for us to listen to the Holy Spirit, obey His Word, and have faith in Him and Him alone for everything. Staying in His will is so critical, because it is in His will that we can hear His voice, feel His presence, overcome sin and evil, and move in His power.

When we experienced the Macedonian Civil War in 2001, we saw that when you go to war, you don't want to be unprepared. You want to know what the enemy is planning. When you fight, you do not hit the air blindly; you get a strategy from Heaven. You get your promises from God to stand on and fight for them to be fulfilled. There are times when you wait on the Lord, but most of the time you press forward in faith, doing what God tells you to do. When brothers and sisters or your pastor tell you, "This is not what God is doing," and suddenly you feel like the door slams shut, you kick that door! It is a lie because it is the opposite of what God told you He was going to do. You know that God spoke, and He will fulfill it!

Hope is 20 days old in Sofia, Bulgaria

Hope is one year old at Ohrid Lake,
where we saw Jesus five years before

Ivan, Hope, and Kiril right before Ivan became ill

Hope is eleven, doing her homeschool work with the cat

Hope's ICS youth group, mostly Americans,
in Skopje, Macedonia, 2010

Hope and Angelina at Vardar River in Skopje, Macedonia, 2010

Hope, Paul Wohlers (American Ambassador to Macedonia, the man in Angelina's dream), his wife Mary, Angelina

Kiril, Netherlands Ambassador to Macedonia, Angelina, 2013, at the Ambassador's home, which is like a castle

Angelina, Kiril's mother, and Hope, 2012

Angelina's mother, 2013

Pastor Glenn and Miss Pat Gilbert, Labor Day 2013, Charleston

Hotdog Ministry in downtown Charleston, Christmas 2013

Prophesying to Pastor Paula White
New Destiny Christian Center, January 2014

Prophesying to Pastor Riva Tims, Majestic Life Church, January 2014

Kiril, Angelina, Pastors Patricia and Mark Estes
North Palm Community Church

Hope's first visit to Washington, D.C., 2015

Angelina, Hope, Pastor Paula White, Kiril - 2017

With Che Ahn in Charleston, 2018

We meet Roberts Liardon, 2018

With Dr. Dondi Costin
President of Charleston Southern University

11

I KILL THE EGYPTIAN

When I was growing up, my security was in money; but after I gave my life to Jesus, He wanted to teach me to have all my security in Him. We lived all the years in Macedonia by faith for His provision, and He was also teaching us to be thankful for all His blessings. Some were free and some were not, but they were all His blessings. The Holy Spirit taught us never to compare ourselves with other people or families. He would give us what we needed not what someone else needed. He would bless us in abundant ways that fit us not other families. And He would never give us something that would hurt us.

While we were missionaries in Macedonia, we didn't have any financial support from a church. God blessed me with a job, which I had to trust God for every week, every month, every year. The money was enough to pay the rent on our apartment, the bills, buy food and clothes, and travel to Bulgaria a few times a year to visit our parents. Through my job, I also met people in the city from every area of life. I took every opportunity to talk to them about Jesus, and they watched me. How I lived spoke to them about what I believed. They were impressed that I loved God first, I respected my husband, I was taking care of my family, and how we raised our daughter. Our lives often speak louder than our words!

In that time, I was spending more time in the world, and Kiril was spending more time with the Lord as he ministered and volunteered. In the back of my mind, I had a lot of thoughts about having a better life. In our refrigerator, we usually only had food for that day. We had to trust God for the next day. In the beginning, this caused me a lot of stress. My flesh didn't want to trust God, and it seemed more money was what would give me peace of mind.

Like every mother, I desired the best for my child, the best for my family. I was looking at other people's lives, people who didn't know God and hadn't seen His glory like I had, but they had material things in abundance. The devil used my weakness and started provoking me to think more and more about these things.

Once I was in the grocery store buying food for dinner. At the cash register, standing in front of me, was a woman I knew. Her cart was so full of food and other products, it was overflowing. I said to God, "See her? She is an unbeliever. She is an adulteress, and look how she can buy all the things she wants. I'm Your child, and I can buy only spaghetti, hamburger, and tomato sauce just for tonight! I left behind everything to serve You. I live according to Your Word. Lord, I just need more peace! Can You please give us more money, so I will not be worried about tomorrow?"

God answered me, "My child, you don't understand. Your peace doesn't come from the material things, but it comes from Me. When you have Me, you have everything." He started to open my mind to understand. "That's why I told you not to compare your life with people in the world. Even if they have material wealth, they do not have My peace. They work hard to earn money and then spend it on things they don't even need. Many times, they work and spend their money on evil things. They are never satisfied, never thankful, never appreciative. They give money to doctors, medications, alcohol, drugs, and all kinds of things that never fulfill and heal them. Their life is endless running after things that will not satisfy them. Be thankful. Be faithful with the little, and I will give you more. Just wait on Me. "

Meanwhile, Bulgaria became a part of the European Union (EU). Many Bulgarians moved to the other European countries for a better life. They were attracted by higher salaries, and Christians did that as well. Many of our friends from Bulgaria moved to France, Germany, Italy, and Spain looking for more. This was a common dream of people coming from post-communist Eastern Europe.

Macedonia was a country in transition, outside the EU and NATO, with a very weak economy. Somewhere in the back of my mind, the thought of going to a more prosperous western country was hiding. The lie was that if God led other Christians to go to other countries, why not us? Doesn't He want to bless us and prosper us as well?

Kiril and I had heard from God that He was going to send us out of Macedonia and that we were going to serve Him in America, but the time seemed to drag on and on. The idea of living in America and being in full-time ministry, instead of having to work to support my family, seemed impossible and distant. The dream was hard to hold onto, but somehow I did.

I began to understand that it is a lie that success, security, and satisfaction are connected with how much money you have. Another big lie is that money is the measure of God's love for you and how much He wants to bless you. Wrong! God's love cannot be measured, and He always wants to bless us. These truths were just beginning to take hold in me when the enemy came in to get me off the track of God's blessings.

One day I got a phone call from a lady I worked for from time to time. She and her husband offered me a month babysitting job on the Spanish island, Ibiza, in the Mediterranean Sea. They said that I would live with their daughter, her son, and her boyfriend, who was a wealthy broker from Marbella, Spain. Their grandson was nine years old. My first reaction was to say no. I couldn't leave my husband and our daughter for a month. Hope was four, and I would miss her too much.

Then I said something that I regretted. "If you pay me double what I earn here in Macedonia for a month, I will come."

To my surprise they said, "No problem," and they would pay my round-trip airplane ticket and pay me for Sundays as well. I agreed. I was excited that finally I would travel in a western country. It was my first time to fly in a plane! I would learn another language and culture. I was twenty-seven.

Kiril supported me in my decision. I had a lot of reasons to do it. I saw a way out. Probably, Spain was our next destination and after that the USA. I wanted something better for my family, and I didn't see how this could happen in Macedonia. Plus, Macedonia was a spiritual desert. We felt isolated and alone. Very few people served the Lord as we did. Nobody encouraged us in what we did for God in Macedonia. *Where is Your promise, Lord? We need to move on!*

There was silence — or I didn't want to listen.

We have to be careful what we ask God for! Whatever we pursue, this is what we get. We must always ask these questions: What is the motive in my heart? Do I like serving God no matter the circumstances, or am I just seeking personal blessing? Am I doing these things for Him or for me?

I went to Ibiza, and Kiril didn't stop me. He was ready to take care of Hope for the whole month of August 2002, and I was ready to go. I was tired of waiting for God to move; it was my turn to move. Everything in my mind made so much sense. Logically, this was so right.

The devil didn't come with something that was obviously wrong and easy to discern. He used the Word of God to trick me. He used the promises of God to provoke me. "God wants to lead you out of Macedonia. This is your chance to do something more for your family! God doesn't want you to suffer anymore! Your time in Macedonia is over."

Doesn't sound so bad, does it?

And who am I not to provide a better future for my family? I believed my taking action would activate God's will and promises in our lives. *Lord, I can't wait for you to arrange our trip to the United States. That is too impossible. But to go to Spain is easy, and maybe later, You will arrange for us to move from Spain to the US.* The red light in my spirit was on. "This is not My way! I'm not leading by material prosperity. Many of My children are falling for that lie. First seek My face. Seek My kingdom first, and everything else will be added to you."

I just had to learn from a mistake, to experience the difference between doing things my way instead of His way. Many of us have to learn this lesson the hard way, just like Moses. He saw how his Hebrew people were oppressed by the Egyptians, and he had a deep desire to deliver them. When he went to check it out, he saw an Egyptian soldier abusing a Jewish brother and killed that Egyptian. Because of that, he had to flee from Egypt and wait forty years before he could carry out his mission to bring the children of Israel out of Egypt. This story shows us that we cannot fulfill God's plan for us through our flesh, in our own thinking. Instead of "killing the Egyptian," we must act by the Holy Spirit, according to God's Word. We must trust God for the right time and the right place. It must be His way not ours.

The month in Ibiza seemed endless. I earned a tremendous amount of money and worked as many hours as I possibly could. The island was the most beautiful place I had ever seen, but inside I was grieving for Kiril and Hope. I missed them so much. I was homesick for our prayers, our worship, and our life together. The battle in me was between my desire to be at home with my family and my desire to make a better life for them.

The family I worked for liked me and my work. The boy and I connected very well. They were Catholics and realized I was a strong Christian through my behavior. I didn't talk to them much, but I did to the boy. As the days passed, they asked me to come again in October and move to Madrid, the capital city of Spain, and work for them full time. They said that after I came in October, they would begin preparing the papers so that Kiril, Hope, and I could live there.

This offer sounded like an answer to my prayers, and Kiril agreed, but it was a perfect example of how the devil will offer you the things you desire just to make sure you are out of God's will and eventually far from Him spiritually.

I was so sure we were doing the right thing. I went to Madrid in October of 2002, and Kiril and Hope went back to Sofia, Bulgaria, to stay in his parents' home until he and Hope could join me. We disobeyed what God had told us, "Do not go back to Bulgaria to live." Kiril went through many attacks and questions about what we were doing, and there was a lot of confusion.

Although I missed my family terribly, the devil was seeing to it that I thought it was worth it. I was paid a large salary and travelled business class to different places in Spain, including the Canary Islands. But deep inside, I knew this was not what I wanted.

One day I was alone in the home in Madrid, flipping through the TV channels. I found *GodTV* and began watching Benny Hinn's program, *This Is Your Day*. As he was speaking, the presence of God came into the room and I started crying. I felt the love of God so powerfully! It shook me, and I heard God ask me, "Angelina, what do you want from Me? What is the desire of your heart?"

I was so convicted. His love was pulling me toward Him, and I heard myself saying, "Lord, forgive me. Forgive me!" The Holy Spirit led me in repentance. I was overwhelmed by the truth that even though I had left my first love and followed my own desires instead of His will, God didn't allow anything bad to happen to me or my family. His love and faithfulness waited patiently for me to come back to Him and return to His path.

I called Kiril that evening, we prayed over the phone, and we knew God wanted me to leave Madrid. A few months later, in January 2003, I traveled to Sofia, and two weeks later we were back in Skopje, Macedonia. We were back on the mission field God called us to, the perfect place to be! He had allowed me to go my own way to see how much better it is to do things His way — no matter how it looks in the natural realm.

We were in Skopje with the same church, the same people, and the same challenges; but the love, joy, and peace was indescribable. I looked at the world with different eyes. I was thankful to God for every simple thing. I was again with my husband and our little daughter. The time apart brought us even closer. I spent more and more time in prayer, seeking God's will and presence more than anything else.

Jesus said, "Enter by the narrow gate; for wide is the gate and broad is the way that leads to destruction, and there are many who go in by it. Because narrow is the gate and difficult is the way which leads to life, and there are few who find it" (Matthew 7:13-14). God's way is straight and narrow, and few are the ones who walk in it.

In the Last Days, many are falling for the same kinds of lies I fell for. I thought God was obligated to give me a certain standard of living, but He already gave me everything I needed when Jesus died on the Cross to pay the price for my sins! After I received His greatest miracle of being born again and was forgiven all my sins, it is now my joy to become like Him and do His works as He leads me.

Now I say to Jesus, "I have been crucified with Christ; it is no longer I who live, but Christ lives in me; and the life which I now live in the flesh I live by faith in the Son of God, who loved me and gave Himself for me" (Galatians 2:20).

12

SAYING GOODBYE TO IVAN

God had spoken to us years before that we would be missionaries to the United States, but when we came back to Skopje, He said, "Stop praying for yourself and start praying for My people in America, because when the time comes for Me to send you there, it's going to be time for great revival. Pray and intercede now, because when you go there, you will not have time to intercede for them. It will be time for ministry."

We asked the Lord why He wanted to send us to the US. For us, the United States was a Christian nation, almost like Heaven. The people there had so many different churches, all kinds of translations of the Bible, many Christian TV channels and programs, preachers and teachers on radio, and a multitude of anointed ministers and ministries. We could not see why He would send us there, especially since it was American ministers like John Osteen and his daughter Lisa who had brought the Gospel to our country of Bulgaria, doing crusades and bringing Bibles in Bulgarian. My first Bible was given by the Gideons in America. I was so happy to have it. It was with me all the time, even when I slept. For all these reasons, we could not understand His purpose.

God answered, "My people in the US have fallen asleep, and I want you to go there and wake them up! They don't believe in Heaven anymore, and what they want is to be blessed here and now. They run after material things and treat Me as a Santa

Claus. I'm not Santa! I'm not fulfilling wishes but providing for your needs. If I don't give them something on their time, they complain and murmur and fall into depression. I'm going to bring a great revival, a great awakening! I'm going to transform them from carnal Christians to spiritual Christians. I'm bringing the Church to where it was at first. I'm bringing restoration of the relationship between Me and My people. This revival will begin now and will last until I come again. I will bring unity to the Church. This revival will be founded and based on My love. Whoever starts flowing in My love will see My glory, My face, and all My promises for their lives will be fulfilled. Whoever refuses to walk in My love will be left behind. No matter how long somebody has been in a church, for twenty or thirty years, it doesn't matter if you don't have love." We kept hearing God speak to believers and unbelievers, "Repent, for the kingdom of God is here."

We realized that America needed Jesus desperately. We started praying and believing that God would do the impossible, that He would make a way where there is no way. We had invested the extra money I got from my work in Spain in Hope's education. We sent her to some private English classes. She started learning English when she was four.

While we prayed in the Spirit, we were seeing visions of standing in front of many people, ministering with prophecy and miracles, and the people were giving their lives to Jesus, being set free and restored. When we would open our eyes, we saw the reality that we were still in the desert, waiting for the promises of God to take place. These visions in the Spirit were so motivating for prayer and to believe that God would do the impossible. It would be a miracle for us to be able to go there!

We had to walk by faith not by sight and to know that

whatever God speaks He will do it. He is faithful, and He wanted to see us be faithful. He would tell us all the wonderful things He had for us and would do through us for other people, but He would warn us over and over, "Stay in My plan in order to see My promises for your life and ministry. Kiril, you have to be strong and ready to continue with Me no matter how difficult it is going to be. Take courage, for I will bless you after I see that you love Me first."

What God was speaking was so serious that we were very much afraid, but He was preparing us for the coming storm. This way, we would not be surprised and we would be prepared. We would know what God wanted from us and would be able to stay with Him on the path He had for us.

God taught us a lot about spiritual warfare. Prayer became a lifestyle of listening to the Holy Spirit. Through the civil war and now in interceding for America, we were more aware than ever that we are in a war, and we must know what our enemy, the devil, is up to. We must pray all the time so that at the right time, the Holy Spirit can tell us the enemy's plans and give us His strategy to overcome.

God told us Satan would try every possible way to keep us from staying in Skopje, using the love Kiril had for his parents to make him go back to Bulgaria and quit every work in Macedonia. The Lord prepared us for every event, showing us how to love the people involved and to continue in His will. This was the only way to defeat the devil. We had the greatest weapon — the love of God!

We also learned that if we only walk in love but not the truth, we will be defeated. We would compromise and fall to temptation (like when I went to Madrid and Kiril went back to Bulgaria). On the other hand, if we stood only on the truth and did not operate in love, we would also be defeated. We saw that we must have a balance in our walk with God and our relationships with each other and the people around us. In this balance of truth and love, we would be able to accomplish all God had for us and stay in His will.

In the summer of 2007, Kiril's father Ivan was turning seventy. We planned to visit his parents and spend time with them. As we were planning our trip, we felt led by God to treat Kiril's father to a mini-vacation in Sozopol, a resort city located at the Black Sea. We wanted to organize a trip where all of us would spend a week there. Ivan's brothers and a sister lived there, so he would be able to spend time with them too. God provided the extra money we needed, and we spent a wonderful week there. Ivan was so happy to see his relatives and to visit the grave of his mother, Kiril's grandmother, who had died a few years earlier and was buried in Sozopol.

Kiril's father was a very loving person. Everybody liked him. He worked as a painter for forty years, and after he retired, he still did some painting. After retirement, he also worked as a handyman in the maintenance of a kindergarten. He was a very active and healthy man. He had gone only once to a hospital. He also was the only person from Kiril's and my families who was helping to support us in what we were doing for God. When we went to visit him in Sofia for Christmas, Easter, New Year's, or vacation during the summer, he would buy the food we liked and would take care of us during our stay. He called us often, even though international calls were very expensive. He wanted to talk to us and to hear how we were doing.

My mother-in-law did not agree with the life we lived as Christians. She only saw us living in a poor country with no future. Kiril's father would say that the most important thing was that we were together, we loved each other, and God would take care of us. He loved me as his daughter, and God gave me what I had missed and did not receive from my own father. I loved him so much, as did Kiril. Hope was in love with him too!

After this wonderful vacation at the Black Sea, we went back to Macedonia. We all agreed we would come to Sofia for Christmas and New Year's, returning to Macedonia a few days later. Christmas was coming closer, and we were led by God that Kiril and Hope would travel earlier. I would join them after I finished all my appointments. This way, they had more time to spend with Kiril's parents.

It was New Year's Eve in Sofia, and as Kiril and I prayed, God gave a prophetic word to Kiril for the coming year. The Holy Spirit usually told us the main things that would take place, or at least some glimpse of what was coming next. That night we were in expectation to hear from God about what was coming. We hoped He would tell us something about going to the US, that the time was near. We had been praying for America for five years!

Instead, all God said was, "Kiril, get ready! In five months, I'm going to take your father home." God said that Ivan had cancer, and soon he would be leaving this Earth. Then God reminded Kiril that, whatever happens, he should not move back to Bulgaria.

We were grieved in our hearts, and after the prayer we went into the living room, where everybody was celebrating. Nothing was visibly wrong with his father. After we went back to Macedonia, I saw that Kiril was in great distress. He was praying day and night. Many times, I saw him lying on the couch, crying.

When we called his parents, they said everything was fine

with them. Then we found out Kiril's uncle died. He was Kiril's mother's brother-in-law. They lived in another city, so Kiril's parents traveled for the funeral. The beginning of February 2008, in one of our conversations over the phone, they mentioned they were going to doctors' appointments. Ivan had lost a lot of weight, and my mother-in-law explained that it was because of a new diet. The Holy Spirit gave Kiril the impression that they were hiding something, and he was still crying and interceding before the Lord for his father. He would tell me, "My spirit grieves. Something is happening with him, and he is not telling me."

On March 20, we celebrated Kiril's birthday. Right after that, he called his father and told him that God had told him something bad was happening to him, that he had been praying for him, and he had better tell him what was happening. Kiril's father broke down in tears. He couldn't hide it anymore. He told Kiril that at the end of January, when they went to the doctor, they found pancreatic and liver cancer. They told him he would live no longer than six months. He asked if Kiril would like to come home and take care of him. There was no doubt that God wanted Kiril to spend his father's last days with him.

Kiril packed his suitcase that evening, and in the morning he was on his way to Sofia. The trip was five hours by bus. He prayed all the way that, when he arrived, his father would still be alive. When Kiril saw his father, he burst into tears. He had lost so much weight, and his skin and eyes were yellow. Kiril felt devastated. He prayed, "Lord I've seen so many people miraculously healed through me, people with tumors, cancer. This is so easy for You! I know, if You say a word, he will be instantly healed. Why my father, Lord? The one I love so much!"

God answered, "Kiril, what will be better for him: to live

longer on the Earth and never to come to repentance, or for Me to take him now, as he goes through cancer and realizes he needs to give his life to me and to be saved? What do you think is better?"

Yes, my father-in-law was an awesome person, but he was so good that he thought he didn't need to repent of his sins and be saved. Kiril would tell him, "Daddy, you have to give your heart to the Lord. You need to repent and receive Jesus Christ as your Savior."

Ivan would answer, "Why do I have to repent? I haven't stolen or murdered, and I'm doing good to everybody."

Kiril would go on to say, "But do you know that because of the sin of Adam and Eve, we all have this sinful nature and come short before the Lord?"

His answer to that was, "If Adam and Eve sinned, they have to repent. I didn't do anything wrong." And the conversation would continue on and on, with no result.

Kiril cried and prayed the whole night, and in the morning, he said to the Lord, "May not my will but Your will be done. After all, everyone's hope as Christians is that one day we will all be together in Heaven."

From that moment on, Kiril had two months of a wonderful time with his father. They would walk in the park and talk about the people they knew and the things that happened when Kiril was a child. Many beautiful memories were brought back. Then, on one of these days, Kiril's father confessed Jesus as his Lord and Savior! He surrendered himself to the Lord completely, praise God! He told Kiril, "I realize now, that I was very good for the people around me, but I wasn't good enough for myself all these years. I was pleasing the people, but my pride kept me so long away from God."

Ivan was going regularly for blood work. The results were terrible. Surgery wasn't an option. The doctors predicted the death to happen in extreme agony and pain, saying that even morphine wouldn't help him. But God was doing miracles! Every time Ivan had pain, Kiril would pray and lay his hands on him, and the pain would go. They never gave him any painkillers!

In April, Hope and I went to visit them during Easter. That was the last time we saw Ivan on Earth. After that, I would talk to Kiril over the phone, and we prayed together, because he was going through the most difficult time in his life. He needed so much to be loved and supported! The biggest pressure was not coming from taking care of his father but from his mother and brother. Kiril's brother was a very angry, jealous, and bitter man. He never loved Kiril, because he always felt like he was competing with Kirl for the inheritance of their parents. There was a time, when Kiril was thirty, that his brother hired people to kill him. He wanted everything for himself. He would come to his parents' home drunk, pressuring them and causing trouble. He accused Kiril of coming to Sofia only because he wanted his father to give him their apartment. All these accusations were meant to hurt.

One day, Jesus came to Kiril's room and said, "Kiril, get ready. In two days, I'm going to take your father to be with Me."

After this visitation, Kiril went to his father's room and opened the door. His father said, "Tell me, Kiril, what Jesus told you. I'm going home soon, right?

Kiril said, "Yes, Daddy. In two days."

He answered, "I'm ready. I'm not afraid. I see Heaven, and I see angels! I just want you to be here next to me." They hugged each other and cried. The love of God and His presence filled the room.

The next day Ivan's condition worsened and they rushed him to the hospital. The doctors gave him a shot and sent him home. The next day, at 1 a.m., I received a call from Kiril saying that the time had come. He asked me to pray, because his father was ready to go any moment. I got up from the bed and went to the window. As I was praying, God gave me an open vision. I saw a golden chariot come from Heaven and take my father-in-law very fast up to Heaven. The gate of Heaven was opened, and I saw how Jesus welcomed him and hugged him. A few minutes later, Kiril called and said that his father had just crossed over.

Kiril, his mum, and the neighbors didn't sleep the whole night. In the morning, they had to prepare for the funeral. Kiril called the funeral agency and helped with the details. He had peace, but his heart was heavy. He felt like his whole world had fallen apart. Hope and I traveled to Sofia the next morning, so we would be there in time for the funeral. When I saw Kiril, he was so tired and worn out! Still, he was very busy, organizing everything. The family gathered together, and everything went well.

Three days after Kiril's dad passed away, God took Kiril to Heaven again. He walked with Jesus on the streets of gold, and he enjoyed every moment in his Lord's wonderful presence. He felt God's love wrapping him like a blanket. Jesus spoke to him about what was coming in his life and ministry. Then He stopped and said, "Kiril, look at this house," and He pointed to it. "Can you see who is inside?"

Kiril saw this beautiful house, and through the window he saw his father! There were some other people in his house, and Jesus gave Kiril understanding that they were people from his family who had come to Heaven earlier. They had come to welcome Ivan to his home in Heaven. Kiril saw that his father looked very healthy, and he wasn't old. Ivan was so happy and excited, he opened the door of his house and ran out onto the streets of gold, jumping for joy.

Kiril watched with Jesus. His father couldn't see Kiril, and Kiril couldn't talk to his father. Then Jesus said," Do you see where your father is and how happy he is now? He is so joyful, he has been doing this since he came here." Then He showed Kiril a plate on the front door of the house. It had both his father's and mother's names on it! Kiril was overwhelmed with love and joy and peace. He hugged Jesus and didn't want to let Him go. He said, "Lord, please let me stay here. I don't want to go back on the Earth. Lord, if You love me, don't send me back!"

Jesus replied, "Kiril, your wife and daughter are waiting for you there."

And he said, "But Lord, they can make it without me. You are going to give them strength!"

"Kiril, it is not that time yet. You must go, because you have work to do for Me. You have ministry, so I want you to do My will on the Earth for the revival I'm going to bring. You haven't seen anything yet! You will see My glory coming down like never before, with signs and miracles. Millions and millions of people will be saved! It's time to go." Jesus gently pushed him back and said, "It's time for you to go back."

Kiril describes how going to Heaven and coming back takes place very quickly. After this experience with the Lord in Heaven, he had complete peace. Even though he misses his father very much, there is no more grief. He knows where he is and how happy he is in Heaven.

13

Coming through the Storm

Kiril's mum was resisting the Lord more than ever. From the time Kiril received the Lord, she was his biggest enemy. When Kiril was a new Christian, an old prophetess prophesied about the great plan of God for his life and ministry, but she said he should be on alert. "Your mum has a leash on her neck, and every time the devil wants to attack you, he will just pull the leash and she will speak what the devil speaks against you!"

It was so painful for Kiril to know that his mother didn't understand that God had to be number one in his life. She was afraid to lose control over him and the relationship they had before God came into his life. She saw how much Kiril loved the Lord, that whatever He would tell him was more important than what she told him, and wherever He would send him, he would go. She wanted to see him prospering in his job, to be recognized and approved by the community like before. She had been so proud of him because he had so many friends, did well in school, then had a wonderful job and so many opportunities. In her eyes, Jesus came and destroyed all that.

When Kiril became a minister of God, his mother became angry with him *and* God. He left his job, gave away everything he had, and began traveling as the Holy Spirit led him. She thought Kiril was brainwashed and deceived. She would say, "You believed in God before. Why do you have to be so extreme in your faith, like a fanatic believer?"

Kiril continued to love and honor his mum, but he didn't obey her. When Jesus came into his heart, his mother lost control over him. Then God put us together and sent us as missionaries to Macedonia. After that, his mother saw him very little, so she took every opportunity to tell Kiril that he was not doing the right thing and would one day come back to her. He was in error and she was right! She hoped that eventually Kiril would come back to Bulgaria and live a "normal life."

Now that her husband was gone, Kiril's mum hoped we would move back and live with her. Ivan had taken care of so many things in their home. My mother in-law didn't even buy groceries! Ivan paid the bills, the taxes, and took care of everything. After he passed away, my mother in-law felt lost. She had to learn how to live by herself and take care of all the things Ivan had done. Kiril and I understood that this was going to take some time, and that she needed some help until she could do everything herself. She was in such grief, she visited Ivan's grave every morning for more than two months. It took almost an hour and a half one way, but she didn't stop going every morning. Kiril stayed for two months to help her.

One day after Ivan passed away, another uncle passed away as well. There was so much death in the family during the last year and a half. Ten members of the family died: uncles, first cousins, and others. It was such an attack of the devil over our family! Most of them died from cancer and had not received Jesus. They were so rebellious against God. When a righteous person dies, God is pleased in their death; but when the unbeliever dies, there is so much grief and depression that comes over the family.

Now two sisters of my mother in-law were mourning for their husbands as well. Another sister had died six years earlier from cancer, and then her son, who was forty-eight, and her daughter at age fifty-one. These two were Kiril's first cousins. It was devastating for everybody in the family. The most common conversations were about the cemetery, the graves, going there, and the funerals. We felt surrounded by death!

Kiril's mum was so lonely without her husband, and then her closest niece died six months later. Her sisters lived in other cities, and their children were close and took care of their mums; but my mother-in-law was alone. Kiril's brother lived in Sofia, but he rarely called to ask how she was doing. When he did call, he made accusations against his father and her. His words made her feel sick and sad. She would tell us that we called and visited much more than Kiril's brother, even though we lived in another country and Kiril's brother was in the same city.

We were going through the difficult time God had warned us about. Kiril's relatives, his family's neighbors, and everybody we knew in Sofia expected Kiril to do what a good son would do: come home and take care of his mum. If he really loved God, was a good Christian man, and a great prophet, he should do the right thing and move his family back to Sofia to live with his mother. Everyone expected him to do this, and they did not understand when he didn't.

People would call him or talk to him in person when he was in Sofia for the two months after his father's passing. They would pressure him to "do the right thing," and he would tell them that he loved his mum, but he and his family had to be where God wanted them to be. God was number one in our lives! He assured his mum and them that we would visit her often, that we would send her money when she needed it, and that we would help her anytime she needed help; but we were not moving back to Sofia.

Through all that pressure and rejection, Kiril really had to die to himself. It was so difficult to do! His love for God was put to the test as he went through this inner battle. The devil was saying, "You have no love. If you don't love your own mother, how are you going to love the others? The Bible says to honor your father and mother. You are not honoring them if you don't move home and take care of her." As usual, Satan was using the Word of God to try to discourage Kiril, bring doubt, and lead him away from God's plan.

Sometimes, Kiril would think, *What if it's God who is speaking to me?* This is common when the devil speaks lies to us. He wants us to doubt that we ever heard from God in the first place. He knows that if he can get us to doubt in our minds that God ever told us something, eventually we will believe his lies and defeat us. Our mind is the battlefield, where we decide to believe God's Word or the devil's lies. What we decide in our mind determines what we will do.

Three and a half months after his father's passing, Kiril bought a bus ticket for Skopje, Macedonia. Even in the last minutes, his mother used accusations and guilt to try to make him stay. She even said, "I will kill myself. I will jump from the seventh floor of the apartment building. How are you going to show love to the other people and serve God, living with the guilt that because of you your mother died? How are you going to live with that?"

Kiril knew this wasn't his mum speaking. It was the enemy. He spoke to her with love, giving her all the reasons she should not kill herself. Finally, he said, "I'm going now. I will go downstairs to wait for you to jump." Of course, she didn't do it, and she came with him to the bus station to say goodbye there. Kiril told her she didn't need to come, but she insisted.

When the bus for Macedonia was about to leave, Kiril said

goodbye to his mum and got on the bus. She stood there with the others, waiting for the bus to leave. When the bus started moving, the driver stopped and told Kiril that his mother had passed out. He knew Kiril and offered to check on his mother, if he didn't mind waiting a few more minutes. Kiril told him to go, that if he got off the bus to see his mum, he might not have the strength to get back on the bus.

As they left the International Bus Station, he cried, for the love of God was filling his heart as he told the Lord He was number one in his life. When the bus crossed the border into Macedonia, the presence of God fell so powerfully on him. God said, "You paid the price! You paid the price to be Mine, to walk in My presence. You paid the price to carry My anointing, and from now on you will see Me working powerfully to fulfill every promise, every word that I have spoken to you and about you."

When Kiril came home that night, he called his mum to find out how she was doing. She shared how she had felt dizzy, had passed out at the bus station, and the people around her gave her water and helped her to sit on a bench. She felt better in a few minutes and went home. Praise the Lord!

14

Preparing in Faith

After Kiril returned to Macedonia, God began to put things in place for us to get to America. He led us to join the International Church of Skopje, a church that was founded as a daughter church of the Evangelical Church of Macedonia for foreigners. The pastor of the church was an American. The members worked in the US Embassy, Netherlands Embassy, various American businesses, and there were other Americans that lived in Skopje. The sermons and the worship were in English. There were Baptists, Presbyterians, and a few Assemblies of God and Charismatics. It was wonderful to see all of them worshiping the Lord together.

God began speaking to us that the time for us to go to America was coming soon. He said, "When the time comes for you to go to the United States, it's going to be a time of a great revival." We were praying more than ever before, asking God to lead us and willing to obey whatever He told us to do. The things He spoke seemed impossible. It was too much for our minds to understand how He would arrange our trip to the US.

The US was always too far away from us. Only certain people could go to the US. You had to have close relatives or close friends to invite you, and still, there was no guarantee you would get a visa. The US Embassy wanted you to prove you would only visit and then would come back to Macedonia. That's why they required you to show them proof that you were employed and owned property in Macedonia, which meant you had strong connections and obligations there. Only sports journalists and people who traveled for business would get visas to visit the US.

As I listened to other people's stories, how they travelled to the US to visit their relatives or were there as students or on business, I couldn't see us in any of those categories of people. Then one day the Lord told me, "Do not listen to what other people say. I will do a miracle for the three of you, and I will be glorified." He wanted us to believe His word before we saw it. He wanted us to declare the victory even if it seemed impossible.

The promise of God seemed wonderful, like it was too good to be true or a dream. He said, "Now is the time for you to show Me that you love Me and that you truly trust Me. Tomorrow you will see that My promise is no longer a promise but a reality."

When we joined the International Church of Skopje (ICS), we strongly believed God was going to use us there, preparing us for our move to America and our ministry there. He always gives you the vision first, and then He gives you the provision. The only thing you must do is believe, so we continued to believe and God used us in places we did not expect.

Our daughter Hope was in elementary public school in Skopje. As a secular school, the children were from families of different faiths and backgrounds, and that made it difficult for the teachers to manage. God enabled us to meet all the parents of the students in Hope's class, which was about twenty-five children. We were constantly in contact with the teachers and the parents to make the educational process easier and more peaceful.

Hope made a huge difference. She quickly earned the love of the two teachers. From the very beginning, she was known by her love and care for the rest of the children. Soon, most of them called her Mama Nadezhda! Kiril and I also had favor with the parents and counseled many of them, as they started feeling comfortable to share their problems and struggles with us. The teachers really appreciated our dedication to help in every way, and they saw great changes in the parents' and the students' attitudes and behavior after we ministered to them. Hope's class became known as the best functioning with the best results.

Then the school asked the parents to help financially and donate our labor to renovate the classroom, to buy new curtains and other materials, so our children could study in a better environment. Most of the parents didn't agree with that, saying that this was a public school and they shouldn't have to give anything. We talked to everyone individually and explained the importance of improving the condition of the classroom, that we were doing this for our children, who would study in the same classroom for four years, spending eight hours a day, five days a week.

In the end, all the parents gave money, and we raised enough to improve the classroom. The teachers were so happy to see how we united for the purpose of improving their workplace. Then, when parents from other classes saw our beautiful classroom, they started raising money for renovation of their classrooms as well. As parents worked together, it directly affected the children's behavior. There was more tolerance and friendship between both parents and students.

We used every opportunity to show Jesus to the adults and to the children. Many times, conflicts were resolved with love and forgiveness between the children and parents. One of the teachers gave her life to the Lord! She told us that she observed our daughter's behavior, how she never acted badly, even when another child offended her. The teacher said that Hope didn't act like an only child. She wasn't selfish and always shared with others, like she grew up in a family with more children.

Hope joined the youth group at ICS when she was eleven. Communicating with the American, English-speaking children helped her to improve her English. Her best friend at the time was the oldest daughter of the Air Force Attaché in the US Embassy in Macedonia. It was always an adventure for Hope to spend time with this family. Very often she would spend the whole weekend at their house, and she wasn't just having fun with her friends; she was also learning a lot about American culture. She also had other American friends, whose parents worked in the US Embassy or had businesses in Macedonia.

After four years of Hope being in public school, Kiril and I were walking in the park one day. The Lord gave Kiril a prophetic word about me. He turned to me and said, "You are going to be Hope's teacher."

I said, "Yes, Lord. I will teach her about You. I will teach her the Bible, so she will know Your Word and grow in the knowledge about You."

Kiril continued, "No, no. I mean you are to be her teacher."

I said, "Lord, I do not understand. What do you mean?" I received the word, which brought joy to my heart, but I truly did not know what God wanted me to do.

Around that time, we met an older American lady at the church. Her name was Ruth Wolters. She was from the Chicago area and had come to Macedonia to teach an American family's children. The mother of the family was Karen Lied. Ms. Ruth told us that she taught the English language in one of the local Macedonian public schools as a volunteer. She was a certified teacher. One day, I asked her if she would like to teach Hope American history during the summer. She gladly agreed, and Hope went once a week to her home.

No matter how impossible it looked, we knew that very soon we would be going to America. God asked us to take a step of faith and begin preparing by investing our time in Hope's education. The first time I brought her to Ms. Ruth's house, I was struck by how cold it was in her house. She always kept the air conditioner very low. Yes, the summer in Macedonia was very hot, around 100-105 degrees Fahrenheit, but we didn't have an air conditioner in our home, so her home seemed unusually cold.

Nevertheless, Ms. Ruth had the most interesting way of teaching American history. It was so well presented, Hope learned easily. I also attended those classes and enjoyed learning about the country that would be our new home.

The summer break was coming to an end, and Hope would start fifth grade at the school she had been attending. Karen came during our American history class in Ms. Ruth's house. She and Ms. Ruth said, "Angelina, do you know that you can teach your daughter at home?" I was surprised to hear that and was confused. How could I take my daughter out of school? In Bulgaria and Macedonia, that was illegal. They challenged me to pray about this and contact them soon. Karen had all the books, from Pre-K through twelfth grade, from an American Christian Curriculum called Sonlight.

Hope and I went home and shared this information with Kiril. As we talked, the Lord reminded us what He had spoken recently in the park, about me being Hope's teacher. Peace, joy, and assurance came to us that this was exactly what God meant. Now I understood!

ANGELINA ISTATKOV

We knew that once we took Hope out of school, there was no turning back. It was a big step of faith to show God that we trusted Him and believed His Word, that this was part of our preparation for our move to the US. We checked Macedonia's laws. Yes, it was illegal to homeschool your children. If the authorities caught you, the penalty was a big fine and/or jail for the parents; but we were determined to do it no matter what it cost us. We believed it wouldn't be long before we left Macedonia for the US.

When it was time to fill out the forms at the school Hope was attending, God gave us wisdom what to write. We wrote that the reason we were taking her out of that school was to move her to a private American school. That was true, but not in the way they thought. We trusted God and prayed that nobody would check up on us.

We asked Karen if she would loan us the materials we needed, and she gave us a box of nearly fifty books for fifth grade. I knew it was going to be a lot of work for Hope, but I also knew that she wanted to study and was hungry for knowledge.

In the beginning, it was very difficult for her, because all the books were in English. I praise God that He brought American Christian moms, whose children were homeschooled as well, to encourage me and help Hope with whatever she needed. Kiril and I were so thankful to God for that year. We all learned a lot, our English improved, and Hope's reading and writing improved also. I still had to work and help her, so she became more independent. The second year, she studied by herself, using the books and other resources available. I would check her work and grade her tests and assignments.

I wasn't aware that I could teach my daughter. It was a miracle! It was another miracle that for these years in Macedonia, God

94

provided the books and materials needed for free. We were now having more time than before to focus on praying and standing before the Lord. Most importantly, our daughter was in a totally Christian environment, and all her friends were from ICS.

During that time, we lived in an apartment in a four-story building in downtown Skopje. Our apartment was on the fourth floor and we had a lot of neighbors. They were curious to know which school Hope attended. They did not see her going to school in the morning, and they wondered about that. They were not satisfied with our answers. Most of the neighbors did not have good intentions, and God revealed that to us. We were attacked by a lot of witchcraft, as some were practicing that in their homes. Witchcraft was common in Macedonia.

When tension was high, the parents of Hope's American friends would pick her up for youth group and bring her home afterwards. The American Embassy vehicles had specific tags, so our neighbors knew that these were Americans, who worked at the US Embassy.

One day, the father of Hope's friend came to pick her up wearing his Air Force uniform. The neighbors were sitting outside on the benches, gossiping. When they saw this man opening the door for our daughter, they were amazed. A few days later, the American ambassador dropped our daughter home after potluck. After that, the neighbors stopped asking questions and even began showing more respect, because they were afraid.

We became friends with most of the people from ICS. We ministered to everybody, regardless of their denominational background. We believed that because they loved and followed Jesus, they would receive prophetic words, prayer, and counsel from the Lord through us.

God was preparing us more and more for our ministry in America. He continued to urge us to pray fervently for His people in the US, and we did this on a daily basis. We prayed that He would awaken the nation and bring His people back to Himself. We spoke to the spirit of mammon and prayed for carnal Christians to repent and live in the Spirit, for revival to come. He said, "I will restore the relationship between the people and Me. I will be their God, and they will be My people."

15

VISAS AND TICKETS

One night, God gave me a dream. He showed me a sign of the time when He would open the door for us to go to the United States. I saw a man dressed in a beige suit. He had blond hair and blue eyes. I was talking to the former Macedonian ambassador in Germany, whom I knew. He pointed to the man in the beige suit and said, "This is the new American ambassador in Macedonia. He is one of you (a Christian). You are going to America, and I see a bright future for your life and ministry that I am not allowed to look into."

The dream was so clear. After I shared it with Kiril, it stayed clearly in our memory. Every two years, there was a new ambassador in the US Embassy in Macedonia. First, there was a woman ambassador. Next, a man with dark hair and mustache. The present ambassador was a bald man. None of them looked like the man I saw in the dream.

One Sunday, when we arrived at ICS, a few ladies from the church greeted us and wanted us to meet the new members. There was a couple sitting in the front row, and as we approached them, I saw the man. He was the man in my dream! We learned that he was the new American ambassador, and we knew our time had come.

God told us to buy a laptop and get on the Internet. We had never had a computer of any kind, and laptops were very expensive; but God arranged for us to pay it off with monthly payments. We went online and discovered *Facebook* and other social media, where Christians all over the world shared their personal experience with God. They were sharing what God spoke to them about the time we live in. Through this, we discovered how the Lord speaks the same word to His people all over the world!

We joined *Facebook* and started connecting with brothers and sisters from the US, sharing the prophetic words God had spoken to us. One of these people was Patricia from Charleston, South Carolina. We sent her birthday greetings through *Facebook* on March 5, 2011. Shortly after, she messaged me and asked for my cell phone number. Kiril and I were walking in the main mall in Skopje, Macedonia, when I received a call from her. She said, "Sister, I see a vision from the Lord right now that you and your family are coming to my home, and God is going to make Charleston a gateway for your life and ministry in the United States."

I exclaimed, "Praise the Lord, dear sister! We know from God that we will go to the US one day, and we are going to serve the Lord there, but we do not know the time or city. We will certainly pray about it!" This is how our friendship started.

We connected on *Skype*, started talking with her on video calls, and we prayed together. Patricia was in a difficult season of her life. She was recovering from a car accident and was lonely. She had very few friends around her and was disconnected from her church. For many months, we were her family and church across the ocean. She told a lot about life in the USA, and we were encouraged that the time for our move was coming soon. Our faith increased that God was going to do a miracle to get the three of us US visas.

In the beginning of 2012, Patricia sent us a personal

invitation. We were not sure if that would be enough to get visas, because we were told that we needed to have an invitation from a church or a ministry. We had connected with many ministers and ministries from different parts of the US, but none of them invited us, because they did not know us personally.

When we received Patricia's invitation, God said, "Make an appointment for an interview at the US Embassy and take this invitation. I will be glorified! I will go before you and will give victory. You just have to smile and speak the truth." We were obedient and made an appointment for the interview.

A few days before the interview, we talked to some Macedonian pastors about it, and they were very pessimistic. They said, "Don't do that! They won't give you visas, because you are applying for the three of you. When they deny your visas, you won't be able to apply again for five years." They shared their experiences. One was invited to visit the US for a two-week conference. He brought papers showing he had a family, owned property, and was employed as a pastor in a church in Macedonia, proving they would come back after their visit to the US. But when he applied for the visa, he was denied.

Fear tried to come on us when we heard these stories, but we refused to receive it. Our whole family was applying, and we didn't own any property or have permanent employment, but we trusted that Jesus was with us and would make it possible. When the day of the interview came, the three of us went to the US Embassy. The embassy waiting room was full of people, not only from Macedonia but from Kosovo. There were many counters, and the persons doing the interviews were behind glass windows. The only way to communicate with the person was by telephones.

We could hear the people before us answering with short

answers of yes and no. We watched their faces after the interview and could tell if they were approved or denied. Not many were leaving with a smile. Many of them brought big folders with papers and documents but left disappointed.

We felt a pressure until the moment it was our turn. They called Kiril's name, and the person interviewing tried to find an interpreter. Then they realized Hope and I spoke English, so they called us too. When I picked up the phone and they asked the first question, I felt the power of the Holy Spirit on me. As I answered, I had great assurance that everything was in God's hands.

Compared to the previous people being interviewed, where they answered with short answers, the person interviewing us asked us interesting questions, such as, "Since you came from an Eastern Orthodox country, how did you become Evangelical Christians?" I told him how I grew up as an atheist, but when I was sixteen-years-old I met Jesus and received Him as my personal Savior. I shared how I met Kiril, who was already in ministry and leading revival services with five to six hundred people. I told him how God put us together and had sent us as missionaries to Macedonia, where we got married, had Hope, and had ministered for nineteen years.

The second question was, "How did you meet the lady who is inviting you?"

At first, I hesitated, thinking, *Lord, should I tell him we met her on Facebook?!* Then I remembered God's instruction, "Just smile and speak the truth." I smiled and answered, "We met her on *Facebook* at a very difficult time for her. We started talking via *Skype*, where we could actually see each other and pray for her." (*Skype* sounded like a more serious way to communicate!) I continued, "We were her only friends at that time. We prayed for her and spoke the Word of God over her life. God restored her spiritually, she went back to church, and she came back to life. She believes that when we arrive in America, God will totally restore her."

In that moment, I looked in this man's eyes and saw tears. We realized the Holy Spirit was touching the heart of this man. He asked, "Why would you like to go to America?"

I boldly answered, "God is sending us there for the revival. It's going to be a great move of God, and He is bringing change in every area of life. We love Americans and believe God is bringing salvation to their nation."

The man pushed the passports on the other side and said, "Come tomorrow to take your passports. Your visas are approved!"

We thanked him, and Kiril grabbed the phone and said, "God bless you." With big smiles on our faces, we left the waiting room. As we walked out, Kiril asked if there were cameras outside, but without waiting for the answer he shouted, "Hallelujah!"

God spoke, and He fulfilled it! He did this amazing miracle, and we were so happy and encouraged for what was coming next. We knew that if He got our visas, He would fulfill every promise He had given us. There was no doubt that we were on our way!

The joy we felt as we left the embassy was overwhelming, and we couldn't hide it. As we walked down the hill where the US Embassy was located, we were praising God with singing, shouting, and dancing all the way home. Now we were unstoppable! With God on our side, we knew nothing was impossible. The time of our wilderness was over, and we were about to enter our Promised Land!

The next day I picked up the passports and saw that they had given us ten-year tourist visas! But God said, "When you step on American land, consider yourself Americans." We knew we would be there longer than ten years. God reveals the end from the beginning, so we trusted Him and prayed about what we should do next.

One Sunday morning, I told the pastor of ICS how God had given us visas. He praised the Lord for the miracle. I told him that this was the good part, but we still needed finances to buy the plane tickets. He said that the church was not able to support us for this trip, but he could make an announcement that we were going to do a fundraising event at our home, sharing our vision of being missionaries to the US. That was a great idea, and I gladly received it. Then he said, "If it's God's will for you to go to America, the people will donate, and you will get the money for the plane tickets. If not, you are not supposed to go."

I did not agree with what he said, because we knew God was sending us to the US and this was the time. When you know what God has spoken, you must believe it and refuse to doubt or receive any discouragement from anyone — even your pastor! I immediately answered, "Dear brother, it is God's will for us to go to the US. There is no doubt about that, and we will see the glory of God when the finances come in!"

The next Sunday morning service, the pastor announced, "Kiril and Angelina received a vision from God to go to the US for the revival. They are inviting everyone who is interested to hear more about that and to support them in this vision, to come to their home on Wednesday at 7 p.m." Afterwards, we thanked him for what he did.

We started preparing for that Wednesday with great excitement! We were expecting many people from the church.

Most of them either worked at the US Embassy or had their own businesses. We got a few calls from those who couldn't come because they would not be in town that day. On Wednesday night, we looked out the window of our apartment, waiting for the people to come; but the only person who came was the nephew of the Ambassador to The Netherlands. He was a young man, a teacher at one of the private schools in the city.

We had a wonderful prayer time with this young man, who was on fire for God, Spirit-filled, and speaking in tongues. This was rare in Macedonia! God spoke to him as Kiril gave a prophetic word. He was extremely blessed and prayed over us. The Lord spoke through him that we would live with a family when we arrived in America. He also sowed a little seed for the trip, which was a beginning.

The thoughts of doubt tried to come into our minds, but God assured us that He had a better plan. A few days later, different individuals and families started contacting us, wanting to come and bring gifts for the trip. We had guests every evening. This was so much better! We had time to share our vision with them and minister to them as well. God opened their hearts, and we raised $4,000 in three weeks!

We bought three round-trip tickets to the US in the summer of 2013. When traveling to the US with a tourist visa, we were required to buy round-trip tickets, but we knew that we were not returning to Macedonia. We would travel on September 19, 2013, from Skopje, Macedonia, to Istanbul, Turkey; then from Istanbul to New York, and finally New York to Charleston, South Carolina. We were so happy to have our plane tickets!

With every victory, our faith grew stronger. God was on the move! We had been making trips to see our families, but now our visits were to say goodbye. Kiril's mum came to Macedonia several days before we left. She tried to convince Kiril to change his mind. She still felt she was losing control over him, but he stood firm that there was no turning back for us.

His mother did come to America in 2016 for three months. During that time, we celebrated Kiril's 50th and Hope's 18th birthdays. His mum was very surprised that in a short time we had found a Christian community that loved us and was taking care of us. She said that in her whole life, she had never experienced such love and peace! Many times, we asked her to move here and live with us, but she wants to stay in Bulgaria. We praise God that Kiril's brother, who lives in Sofia with his family, takes care of her now.

My parents had moved from the city to a house they built in the country. Today, they are members of an evangelical church in Pernik. We talk often over *Skype*, but they are not planning to come here either. They knew the prophecy that God was going to send us to America for the Great Revival, and they saw the glory of God for us!

Meanwhile, the summer was closing quickly and soon September came. We said our last, tearful goodbyes. Since we were renting an apartment and paying bills, we made sure that we paid everything and didn't owe anything. The day before the trip, we had $20 in our pocket, two suitcases, and a cat in its carrier. We were ready to go! God told me, "Do not talk about money to anybody."

I said, "But Lord, how are we going to get to the airport in the morning? The taxi costs at least $40. Kiril and I are crazy for You, and we can go with nothing anywhere, but we have a daughter who is fifteen years old. What if she gets hungry on the way or she needs something?"

The Lord rebuked me, "Do you think you are a better parent than Me? She is first My daughter and then yours." I repented!

A few minutes later, a brother, who was an American businessman in Macedonia, called me and asked if we needed a ride to the airport in the morning. I answered, "Yes, we appreciate that very much. You hear very well from the Lord." I couldn't tell him that we didn't have the money to get a taxi. He arrived early in the morning with his fourteen-year-old daughter, and they drove us to the airport.

We were very excited that we are leaving Macedonia and going to our new home in the United States of America. We knew it was going to be very challenging, but there was an overwhelming trust in our hearts. It was time for boarding, and we hugged our American friend and his daughter. We were ready to step on the escalator and go to passport control. Just as we were stepping to go up, our friend said, "Wait! Wait! I almost forgot to give you this." He reached into his pocket, took out a little envelope, and said that it was a love letter from his daughter to our daughter. He handed it to Hope, and we stepped on the escalator. As we were going up, Hope opened the letter and saw $200 cash in it!

16

COMING TO AMERICA

The first time God spoke to Kiril and me that He would send us to the United States was when we were on the bus to Macedonia in 1994. Now, almost twenty years later, what He had spoken to us was being fulfilled. He had provided everything we needed to get to the USA and for our first days there. Our God is faithful and true! He had kept us going in the right direction, even when we didn't understand, even when we made mistakes, and now we were seeing His glory like never before.

Our trip to America was an historic time for all of us. We were stepping into the unknown, into a new country, learning a new language, experiencing a people with a different culture. We knew only Patricia. We knew she could probably have us in her home for only a short time before we would have to move out. We didn't know how God would do it, but we were sure He would find us a place to live. We knew He would take care of everything. All we had to do was what we had always done: hear and obey.

Kiril had flown to Germany to minister years before, and I had flown to Spain, but this was Hope's first time to travel by airplane. It was a great experience for her. When the plane took off from Skopje, Macedonia, we felt like we were leaving a heavy and dark spiritual atmosphere, which we knew was over the city and the country. At once, we felt lighter, like a great weight was removed. Praise the Lord!

Our first flight to Istanbul, Turkey, was short. When we arrived, we had to go through customs before boarding our flight to New York. The line was moving slowly, and the policemen were rude and strict with everybody. They checked our visas and asked us a lot of questions, including if we knew where we were going in the US and how long we were planning to stay. Finally, we boarded the plane and moved to the very back to find our seats. We had our cat in a carrier and gave her sleep medicine, then put the carrier at our feet. We knew the flight was about ten hours, thirty minutes, but we also heard that Turkish Airlines were kind and the service was good. That proved true! They were known for serving good size portions of delicious food. We enjoyed it!

During the flight, the Lord told us to pray for our future material blessings and financial support for fifteen minutes only. We prayed over our finances for fifteen minutes and then said, "Amen." Even today, our ministry has always been well supported by the gifts and offerings of people we minister to; so again, God spoke, and He fulfilled it.

The moment after we said amen, Kiril had a vision of a cloud, like the cloud of glory, over the plane. It was moving with us. When we arrived in New York, God continued the vision, and the cloud of glory covered the United States from coast to coast. The Lord said, "Many people are speaking evil against this nation. Many say My wrath is coming, that I will destroy this nation; but that is a lie of the devil! I love America, and I am going to bring salvation to this nation. You are going to see millions and millions of people saved and thousands and thousands will be healed. You are going to see more people going to Heaven than those who perish and go to Hell. I am bringing a great revival to the USA!" Amen!

We landed at JFK Airport in New York and had a layover for twenty-one hours. That was a long time, and we stayed at the airport the whole time. We found Terminal 5, where we would catch our next flight, and started looking around. We saw that most of the policemen and security guards would go to Dunkin' Donuts to eat, just like we had seen in the American movies. We met a lot of people coming and going in the terminal. When we got sleepy, we would sleep in shifts, because of watching the luggage and the cat.

In the morning, we were hungry. We sat on a bench, and a lady from Puerto Rico sat next to Hope. The lady had missed her flight, so she had a long time to wait for the next plane. We told her about how God had sent us to America for the revival. We led this lady in prayer and she rededicated her life to God. She was so blessed and touched. She was happy that she missed her flight! Then she left for a few minutes and came back with a whole bag of donuts and other pastries from Dunkin' Donuts. She gave the bag to Hope and told her that the Lord had led her to buy her breakfast. It was so nice of her to do that — especially since she didn't know we were so hungry! We met other people and ministers while we were waiting for our plane. They asked us why we came to the US, and we ministered to all of them. Praise the Lord!

Finally, around 12:30 p.m., we got on the plane to Charleston, South Carolina. The flight attendant said, "Turn off all the Blackberries, blueberries, strawberries, and any berries, please." LOL! We knew we were home. The official language and formality was gone. People were friendly and nice, and the flight was so enjoyable. We were watching from the windows, and all we could see was blue water and green land. It was so beautiful!

Many years ago, God spoke to us that He would send us to

a place where there would be a lot of palm trees and a warm climate. When we arrived in South Carolina, we found out that the palmetto tree was even on the state flag! The pollution in Eastern Europe, Bulgaria, and Macedonia — in all Eastern Europe — was very bad. The traffic and the factories were polluting the air in the cities. When we arrived in Charleston, we were amazed at the clean air, the many rivers, the ocean, and the green trees. It was such a big difference from the cities of concrete and small park areas, where we used to live. We were praising and thanking God for everything.

The joy of coming to the place God promised us was indescribable. Patricia would pick us up at the airport in Charleston. When we landed, we called her, and she pulled her car into the arrival lane. She slowly got out of her car and had difficulty lifting her head, but she gave us hugs. After we put the suitcases in the trunk, we left the airport. She was so happy to finally see us, and we were so excited to meet her too. Her apartment was in Goose Creek, which is about twenty minutes from the airport.

We gazed out the windows of her car in amazement. Everything was so new, unknown, and very different from what we were used to. The streets were wide, the traffic lights were hanging, everything looked bigger, and the distances from one place to the other were longer. Patricia told us the names of every restaurant we passed. She told us that she didn't have any food at home, so we went to Walmart before arriving at her apartment. She also told us that she didn't have any money, so we bought food and put gas in her car. When we told her that $200 was all we had, she was a little disturbed. She had warned us to come with at least two or three thousand dollars. All we knew was that God had a plan, and we had to trust Him.

We had peace because we had prayed for fifteen minutes about our finances just as God had told us, but we also knew we needed His quick intervention. He had to make a way where there seemed to be no way. Patricia didn't have a lot of friends and lived a life of isolation, but we didn't want to be a burden to her. We couldn't count on her, and we knew we had to connect with a church family in Charleston as soon as possible.

As Patricia was introducing us to life in America from her point of view, we were praying for God to lead us forward. What next, Lord? Her apartment had only one bedroom, and she was afraid her property manager would not allow her to have guests for more than two weeks. Even if we did have enough money for rent, we were foreigners in America on tourist visas. Again, we needed God to make a way where there was no way!

Patricia took us to church on Sunday morning, which was two days after we arrived in the US. Such a joy came to us that we would go to church for the first time in America and that we were able to meet our brothers and sisters in Christ. At that time, Kiril didn't speak or understand English at all, so I translated for him.

The transition for Hope was easy, but for Kiril and I, not so much! The language barrier was hard for him, especially since he is a very outgoing person. He likes to talk and joke with people, and he prophesies almost all the time. It was so difficult for him the first few months, but God gave me the ability to translate for him. We started to flow together in love and harmony as we ministered to the people. It's a wonderful flow when there is unity in the Spirit! We heard the same things, spoke the same things, and one of us would start a sentence and the other would finish it. It's an amazing experience!

In that time, I realized that I wasn't only translating what

Kiril spoke prophetically, but there was also such an alignment with the Spirit of God. I could feel the love of God flowing through me. I could understand the heart of God for the people on a new and totally different level. It was not just ministry but an expression of our relationship with God.

Sometimes Kiril felt guilty for not learning English before we came to the US, but a prophetess said to him shortly after we arrived, "God is going to use the fact that you don't understand what the others are saying. Before you hear the translation, the Holy Spirit will reveal what is truly in their hearts and minds." God was giving Kiril a powerful discernment, and the people were amazed how God was revealing to him what they were going through. That's why, many times, Kiril asks the people to tell their stories *after* the prophetic word, so they can be encouraged that God knows them very well.

That Sunday morning, September 22, 2013, we arrived at New Day Church in Summerville. As we walked toward the building, we felt the love of God. When we came in, we were invited to go to a prophetic room before the service started. We did, and some sisters in Christ prophesied over us, confirming our calling and the importance for us to be in America for the revival. We were very encouraged! Then we walked into the sanctuary.

While we were greeting the people around us, God gave us a word for one couple. The power of God came on them while Kiril prophesied over them. They confirmed the prophetic word and were very encouraged. We enjoyed the worship and the sermon so much, and after the service, the pastor's wife and other members came to meet us. We shared with them why God had sent us to the US. They welcomed us and encouraged us to move forward. We also met the Hess family, who were ministers at the church. They invited us for dinner one day during the week. As we talked with them, we asked for an opportunity to minister in the church, but they told us that we had to attend the church for at least six months first. We knew from God we didn't have that much time and wondered how God would work this out.

The visit in New Day Church gave us a real hope and great refreshing. I called the pastor's wife and explained to her the situation with Patricia and that we needed to move out of her home. I asked if we could move to someone else's home while we adjust to our new country. She sounded very encouraging and promised to talk to her husband. They would see what they could do to help us. She did tell me that they currently had visitors in their house, otherwise they would gladly have us.

We were so pressed by the circumstances, but were trusting the Lord for His plan. When the $200 cash was gone, Patricia said, "Since we don't have any food at home, I will take you to a ministry in the inner city of North Charleston to pick up some groceries. They know me there, so I will call and make an appointment." We were very hungry and a little disappointed. On our way to that place, Patricia told us not to talk to anybody, because she felt ashamed for inviting us to America. She really did not understand how big a part she played in God's plan to get us to America!

When we arrived, there was a black woman at the door who was very welcoming. We didn't know that this place was a church, so when we were introduced to Glenn Gilbert, we didn't know he was the pastor. He also had come to the door and greeted us. He asked who we were and where we came from. As we walked to what was the sanctuary, we shared why we were in the US and all the miracles God did to get us here. We told him the visions and prophetic words God had spoken to prepare us for the revival in America.

The presence of God fell upon us all, and Pastor Glenn started crying. While we were talking, other volunteers in the church joined us. Kiril prayed for each one as the Holy Spirit led him. As he prophesied, many were slain in the Spirit, delivered, and healed. We didn't know any of them, but God knew them! It was such an encouragement. Their faith was increased through the prophetic word.

While we ministered to the people, we forgot we were hungry. We were so happy to see what God was doing for them. Pastor Glenn was so excited for what he saw, heard, and experienced. He invited us to minster on Sunday morning and share our testimony. He explained that usually he didn't invite other people to speak on Sunday, but the Lord told him to invite us.

We gladly accepted the invitation. He asked us to pray for his wife, Patricia (we all called her Ms. Pat), and their daughter, Page, who was visiting from Texas. We had an awesome time together. They gave us a lot of food and said they would bring more later that day. We left happy and expecting to see what God had in store. When Pastor Glenn and Ms. Pat came to the apartment that day to bring more food, they invited us and Patricia to come to their home for dinner on Friday evening. We were overjoyed! That was a great opportunity to share more prophetic words and testimonies of God's faithfulness through the years.

We arrived at their home for dinner, ate delicious hamburgers, and had a wonderful time. God prompted us to share that we needed to move out of Patricia's home as soon as possible, and Pastor Glenn consulted with Ms. Pat. She said we could stay with them as long as the three of us were okay sharing one bedroom. Their house had two bedrooms and one bathroom. We could stay until our legal challenges were resolved about staying permanently. We didn't mind staying in one bedroom and were so grateful, but we said we should pray about it before giving them an answer. Before we left, they also blessed us with some clothes.

The next morning, God awoke Kiril around 4 a.m. and told him that this offer to stay at the Gilbert's was from Him. I called Pastor Glenn around 7 a.m. and told him we agreed to come and live with them. As though they were waiting on our call, ten minutes later they came to Patricia's apartment to pick us up. The love we saw in him and through him encouraged us so much!

We thanked Patricia for everything she had done for us. We let her know that we really appreciated her obedience to invite us to America and host us in her home for two weeks. We also gave her the cat we brought from Macedonia as a gift! Our cat had connected with her so well, even from the first day, and the cat would keep her company.

Overnight, we had a family, a home, a church — everything we needed!

It was now October 10, 2013.

17

REVIVAL FIRE IN AMERICA

The name of our new church was Celebration Station. It was located on Reynolds Avenue in North Charleston, a street once known for prostitution. The navy base was close by, so it used to be a place for drinking and partying. By the time we moved there, there were seven or eight churches just on that street. Celebration Station's main focus was to distribute groceries and clothes to the neighborhood. Pastor Glenn and Ms. Pat had run the church and ministry for about twenty years.

Celebration Station was open every day of the week. People would usually come there to get their groceries and clothes. Moving to the Gilbert's house, we were invited to go with them to the church every day. We would leave the house at 7 a.m. with Pastor Glenn. After the people got their food and clothing, they would come to the sanctuary, and we prayed for them. Most days, there were between thirty and forty people there. They were all expectantly waiting in line for their turn.

We prayed for each one individually. God delivered people from demonic oppression and depression, and He healed the sick who had been suffering from cancer, AIDs, and other illnesses. Drug addicts, alcoholics, and prostitutes came for God's intervention in their lives. The love of God was pouring out without measure! The people were coming and confessing their sins, the Holy Spirit was setting them free, and they received the will of God for their lives. They would leave strong and ready to serve the Lord.

God's timing for us to find Pastor Glenn and Ms. Pat was perfect. Ms. Pat had had breast cancer three years before and had had a very difficult time with chemotherapy and recovery from the surgery. She went through a lot of rejection and abandonment from people as well. Most of her friends left when they heard she had cancer. Her daughter, her son-in-law, and their four children left Charleston and Celebration Station overnight. That was a time of great distress for her and Pastor Glenn. She was mostly at home alone while he took care of the food ministry with the help of volunteers. Many times, she couldn't go to the kitchen to get food or water. Then, just two months before God brought us into their lives, they received the news that the cancer had come back, and another surgery was scheduled. They both were discouraged. If she had to go through the same thing again, they would have to close the church.

After we moved into their house, we were led to pray for Ms. Pat a lot and show her love. Hope was always with her: in the house, in the car, at the store, and at the church. The surgery went well, and the side effects from chemotherapy were minimal. Ms. Pat was on her feet much sooner than before, doing administrative work at the church and cooking for the volunteers twice a week.

We knew God wanted us to be in their home and church, but we soon saw this other reason that He put us together. Hope helped Ms. Pat in the office while doing her schoolwork. We helped them in the ministry and the home while Ms. Pat recovered, and God really blessed all of us. She cooked for us, and we loved the time we spent around the dinner table, sharing God's faithfulness in our lives. Also, as Kiril and I were ministering to people, God led some to begin supporting us financially. This way, we could pay our part of the bills for electricity and water in the house. We were happy to do that!

As we ministered in the sanctuary at Celebration Station, we never knew who was going to come through the door. One day a tall, black man came in. He probably was in his forties. Pastor Glenn was there as well. The man walked down the aisle and said, "Please pray for me. I feel very bad." Kiril tried to put his hands on his head, but he was too tall; so, Kiril stepped on a chair. Even before he laid his hands on him, the man dropped down to the floor like a tree. He hit the floor, and Kiril started commanding the devil to leave this man. He put a hand on his head and his other hand on his stomach. I was translating every word, but the man wasn't moving or making any noise. He was totally lifeless! For a moment, I was afraid, and I told Kiril that he might die. Kiril assured me that he was okay, that God was delivering him.

We continued to pray, and around fifteen minutes later, the man opened his eyes. He looked around and asked, "Who are you, and where am I?"

Pastor Glenn told him how he had come into the sanctuary and had asked for prayer. The man didn't remember anything that had happened in the last few days. He confessed that he was taking drugs. At that moment, he was totally sober, and we led him in prayer to receive Jesus as his personal Savior.

Another man named Willy came for prayer with his two neighbors. Kiril was about to lay hands on him, but he asked to pray just holding hands. We all held hands, and Kiril said a very common prayer, "Lord, we thank You for this day. We thank You that You are among us." Suddenly, we heard, "Boom!" We opened our eyes and saw this man on the floor! Kiril leaned down and laid hands on him, commanding every spirit of sickness, oppression, and depression to go.

The man said he felt energy going through his whole body.

He stood up and ran around the sanctuary, rejoicing and giving praise to God. He stopped at the cross on the wall and began praying. He said, "I'm leaving my sins here." He turned to us and said, "My children, I brought you here to America in a miraculous way." Then he stopped and said, "What I am saying?" We encouraged him to continue, that these were not his words but God's words. As he continued, it was amazing to see this man, who had just been delivered, begin to prophesy about the mighty works of God.

Willy's two neighbors had gotten scared when he fell to the floor, so they had left; but a few days later they came again to receive prayer. After Willy had left, Pastor Glenn and Ms. Pat told us that he had had AIDs for fifteen years, which is why he was so slim and weak. Willy came back a month later, and he was crying for joy. "They don't understand! They don't understand! The doctors can't explain how this could happen!" We asked him what happened.

Willy told us that there was a shooting in the neighborhood, and he got shot four times in his legs and was rushed to the hospital. First, the doctors found a bullet wound, but no bullets were found in his legs. Also, there was no a place where the bullet went through his legs. They ran lots of tests and found out that the AIDS was gone. He also had had liver cancer, and it was gone. They had to repeat some of the tests, because they wanted to make sure they had not made a mistake.

The doctor asked Willy how this was possible, and he said that since he had come for prayer, he had gained weight and felt stronger. He said, "These crazy Bulgarians prayed for me. I didn't even understand what this man was saying, but I hit the floor and this energy went through my whole body. I stood up and ran around the sanctuary!"

One morning, a white lady from the hood rushed in. I'll call her Mary. She was frightened and told us that her boyfriend was abusing her physically and emotionally. She asked me to tell Kiril not to call the police and report it, because she was afraid her boyfriend would find out and kill her. We assured her that we would not call the police, but we would pray for her and stand against this spirit of fear and control.

Mary told us that she had been raped when she was six years old, and later in her life she was always falling into abusive relationships. For sixty years, she had been in this cycle of demonic bondage. She showed us the bruises on her body and told us her face was numb on one side. After talking with us for a while, she became calmer and we started to pray for her. Kiril commanded the devil to take his hands off her and for the spirit of fear and control to leave, in Jesus' name. Mary fell on the floor and shouted the name of Jesus while praying in tongues. When she finally stood up, we told her, "Mary, you have the authority to stop that abuse. In Jesus' name, you have the power to say, 'No! You can't hurt me!'" These words hit her powerfully.

She said yes and ran to the telephone in the hallway of the church. She called the police and reported her boyfriend for domestic violence, trauma, and the injuries. The police and the ambulance were at the door of the church in a few minutes. She had to write down everything that had happened to her. The doctor wrote a report on her physical injuries from the abuse. We gave her a hug, and they took her.

Some people at the church said that statistics show that the victim always goes back to the abuser. We said, "Not this time!" Mary received spiritual deliverance and she believed that she was free. Two months later, I received a call at the church office from Mary. She sounded so happy! She told me that she lived in an apartment in a nursing home in another city, that she is surrounded by Christians, and she goes to church. Jesus gave her a new life!

> *Then Jesus said to those Jews who believed Him, "If you abide in My word, you are My disciples indeed. **And you shall know the truth, and the truth shall make you free.**"*
>
> *They answered Him, "We are Abraham's descendants, and have never been in bondage to anyone. How can You say, 'You will be made free'?"*
>
> *Jesus answered them, "Most assuredly, I say to you, whoever commits sin is a slave of sin.*
>
> *And a slave does not abide in the house forever, but a son abides forever. **Therefore if the Son makes you free, you shall be free indeed.***
>
> *John 8:31-36 (emphasis mine)*

On some days, we would pray for close to forty people, and the number of miracle stories — of salvations, physical and emotional healings, deliverances from all kinds of addictions — are too numerous to write in this book. God also brought people from other churches to be set free and restored. We organized revival services and invited other churches to join with us. In one service, we had people from eleven different churches. Then we were invited to minister in their churches and bring the fire of revival there!

Pastor Arthur Jenkins of Saint James Episcopal Church called and asked if Kiril and I would come and lead a healing service in his church. I wanted to make sure he knew how the Lord worked through us, so I asked, "Brother, are you sure you want us to come? We pray in tongues, we lay our hands on the people and pray for deliverance as well as healing. You might see some people fall on the floor. Do you agree with this?"

He answered, "Whatever the Holy Spirit wants to do, I'm open to receive."

At that service, I shared a short testimony of how and why God sent us to the US, then Kiril and I started ministering to the people individually. Kiril laid hands on one lady, who was slain in the Spirit, and everybody clapped their hands! They had high expectations for God to touch them. Another lady said she and her husband had been trying to have a baby for long time and were thinking about adoption. Kiril prayed for her healing, breaking generational curses. He told her that if they wanted to adopt a child, it was their choice; but God was going to give them their own child. A few weeks later, this sister wrote to us that she was pregnant! Now they have a wonderful boy. Praise the Lord!

Kiril prayed for one woman to be delivered, and suddenly she was praying in tongues. She was so loud, and she wouldn't stop! Her prayer language was flowing like a fountain out of her. Her friends who had brought her were amazed, clapping their hands with joy. We didn't quite understand why they were so excited, because we witnessed this every day; but they said she had never prayed in tongues before. God just baptized that woman with His Spirit and fire!

We had the privilege to minister in Palmetto Land Baptist Church in Summerville with Pastor Gene Carpenter and his son Pastor Daniel Carpenter. It was so amazing how God opened the door for the ministry there. The way Pastor Daniel introduced Kiril as his brother from Bulgaria and the love he showed was the key that opened the hearts of the people to accept the blessing and the prophetic word.

We praise the Lord for divine appointments and connections! It was such a blessing to visit New Destiny Christian Center and meet Pastor Paula White. On our way to the church, the Lord showed Kiril a vision of lightning from Heaven hitting the church. We went there in January 2014 to visit, and Pastor Paula invited us on the platform. She asked us how and why we came to the US. We shared a short testimony and Kiril prophesied to Pastor Paula and to the church. It's such an honor to have kingdom friendships!

In 2015, we met Heidi Baker in Savannah, Georgia, at Iris Conference. She gave us huge hugs, welcomed us, and thanked us for our obedience to come to the US and serve the Lord here. "America needs revival," she said.

In 2018, we had the opportunity to meet our friend and brother in Christ, Roberts Liardon. God had used him to bring the message of Heaven to Bulgaria during the revival there.

After four years of ministering at Celebration Station, the Lord led us to move to North Palm Community Church. Pastor Mark and Patricia Estes opened not only their hearts but also recognized us as a ministry of their church family. They have become an important part of the revival in the city of Charleston by promoting unity in the body of Christ, and we were thrilled when they commissioned us as apostles to the body of Christ. We are so happy to have a home church that loves and supports us.

A FINAL WORD

We praise the Lord that He brought us to the US with the fire of revival in our hearts for this nation. We all know that we live in the last days before the return of our Lord and Savior, Jesus Christ. Again, as I wrote earlier in this book, God says that this last move (the revival) will begin in the USA and spread around the world. In this move, we will see the manifestation of the Holy Spirit like never before. Millions will be saved, thousands will be healed, and dead people will be raised.

God says that this move is of the love of God. Those who will flow in His love will love Him and their neighbor (Matthew 22:37-39). They will see the glory of God like never before and will be part of His work in this last move! Those who will not accept His love will be left behind. We are encouraging you to love the Lord and love one another, and you will fulfill all the Scriptures!

We believe God is going to connect us with all the people of God in the US who love the Lord, love others, and are sharing the vision of unity in the body of Christ. We are excited about all He has done, is doing, and will do in the future. If there is one thing we have seen over and over again: *God Spoke — And He Fulfilled It!*

How to Contact the Istatkovs

843-751-8227

kirilistatkovministries@gmail.com

P. O. Box 22572
Charleston, SC 29413

CPSIA information can be obtained
at www.ICGtesting.com
Printed in the USA
FFHW010344130319
50966452-56393FF